Like
Trees
That
Grow
Beside
a Stream

Like
Trees
That
Grow
Beside
a Stream

Praying through the Psalms

Donald E. Collins

UPPER
ROOM BOOKS

N a s h v i l l e

Like Trees That Grow Beside a Stream

Excerpt from *Something Beautiful for God: Mother Teresa of Calcutta* by Malcolm Muggeridge, Collins/Fontana Books. Used by permission of Collins Publishers.

Excerpt from *The Irony of American History* by Reinhold Niebuhr. Copyright 1952 Charles Scribner's Sons; copyright renewed © 1980 Ursula Niebuhr. Reprinted with permission of Charles Scribner's Sons, an imprint of Macmillan Publishing Company.

Excerpts from *The Way of the Heart* by Henri J.M. Nouwen. Copyright © 1981 by Henri J.M. Nouwen. Reprinted by permission of HarperCollins Publishers.

Excerpt from *Gitanjali* by Rabindranath Tagore. (New York: Collier Books/Macmillan, 1971) Used by permission of Macmillan Publishing Company and Macmillan (London) Ltd.

Excerpt from *Waiting for God* by Simone Weil. Used by permission of G.P. Putnam's Sons.

Cover design: Jim Bateman
Cover photograph: Fred Sieb
Book design: Harriette Bateman
First Printing: March 1991 (7)
ISBN 0-8358-0630-8
Library of Congress Catalog Card Number: 90-71864

Printed in the United States of America

For

Liz

who called forth

the monk in me

Contents

CONTENTS

CONTENTS

CONTENTS

Preface

When Pope John XXIII "opened the windows" of the Roman Catholic Church by convening the Second Vatican Council in 1962, the fresh air which began blowing through Catholicism brought new ideas to mainstream Protestant churches as well. Dialogues already in progress between Catholic and Protestant theologians, liturgical and biblical scholars took on new life and spread rapidly through both traditions.

One of the happy results for Protestants was the rediscovery of the importance of spiritual formation, which had been all but forgotten following the animosities of the Reformation and Counter-Reformation. Some important spiritual practices had fallen into decline even among Catholics and, for the most part, were kept alive only in monastic communities.

Among the most important of these practices was *lectio divina*, divine reading. A vital part of Christian spirituality since the days of the early church, *lectio divina*, or more briefly *lectio*, has been the backbone of monastic prayer for fifteen hundred years. In our time it is coming to be known simply as "praying scripture."

Lectio is based on the simple idea that the Bible is meant to be *prayed* as well as read, studied, and expounded upon. The scriptures are thus to be understood as more than a collection of religious history and wisdom. Likewise, they are also more than a springboard for preaching, theological debate, or moral persuasion. The Bible is also a manual for private prayer. In order to understand scripture in this way, we must be open to experience our Judeo-Christian tradition as something more than a system of rational beliefs, bureaucratic structures, and antiseptic liturgical practices, which our generation has inherited as a result of the influence of Western culture over the past one thousand years.

John S. Dunne in his book, *The Way of All the Earth* has described the phenomenon of "passing over" to another culture or religion and then "coming back" to one's own culture or religion with new insight.[1] In a sense, this happened in the 1960s and 1970s for those who explored the philosophical and religious thought of the East and in the process began to find new meaning in their own Western roots. The availability of relatively inexpensive international travel has made it possible for many to quite literally cross over into the "old world" and return with new insight and understanding of their own culture. In a similar way, clergy and laypersons who have had the opportunity to visit the Holy Land for any length of time come home with new insights into their own religious traditions.

Such a crossing over and coming back ought to be and usually is a humbling experience. This is especially true for Protestants, who have a tendency to think that their roots as a religious people go back only a few hundred years. In 1984 when I tried to engage members of a United Methodist congregation in a conversation around the fact that the bicentennial of American Methodism that year represented only ten percent of their history as Christians, all I got were blank stares. I suggested that, spiritually speaking, they were Anglicans before they were Methodists, and prior to that they were Roman Catholics, and prior to that they were Jews.

Our religious and cultural provincialism can be a major stumbling block to spiritual growth. When one speaks to Protestants about "spiritual formation," the response, often unspoken, is one of suspicion because it sounds "Catholic." And the fact that many of our spiritual traditions and practices go back to roots in Judaism only adds to our reluctance to open ourselves to ideas which we would otherwise find both interesting and helpful.

As Christians, we need to nurture an appreciation of our spiritual roots in the early church and in Judaism. We need to go beyond the rational assumptions of Western Christianity to appreciate the more affective experiences of spirituality in the Eastern world, where our Judeo-Christian tradition has its roots.

Nevertheless, we live in a time when many Christians have a genuine sense that something is missing in their lives and are often aware that what is missing is spiritual in nature. That missing element is surely one of the important factors that has contributed to the decline of mainstream denominations in the past few decades. At the same time, the growth of evangelical churches during the same period is due, at least in part, to the fact that evangelical Christianity may offer a spirituality which is more affective in character.

There is an obvious need for the restoration of a greater spiritual vitality in mainstream Christianity. But the answer will not be found in a compromise of biblical and theological integrity. Rather, we need to, as mainstream Christians, cross over to a new appreciation of our own spiritual heritage, including the vital tradition of spiritual formation. This task can only be accomplished by overcoming some of the religious and cultural provincialism and prejudice which keep us from looking more deeply into the roots of our faith. As Dom John Main has said:

> This means transferring our conscious hopes for a renewal of the church's relevance and effectiveness in the world from politics to prayer, from mind to heart, from committees to communities, and from preaching to silence.[2]

It is my hope that this book will make a small contribution toward that end by helping contemporary Christians to discover the simple, yet profound practice of praying scripture. This ancient form of Christian prayer offers great potential for those in our time who yearn for a deeper spiritual maturity.

What better place to begin the practice of praying scripture than the Book of Psalms, which has been the prayer book of the Bible for countless generations. In spite of their origin in a religious and cultural setting vastly different from our own, the Psalms speak to us with a universal longing for God. Without pretense or superficiality, they address the very human questions with which people in every generation struggle.

Unless otherwise noted, all biblical references in this book are from the Today's English Version of the Bible (TEV). While the TEV may lack some of the poetic quality of the King James Version or the New Revised Standard Version, it is not so modern that its language loses a sense of respect and holiness. It is written in contemporary English, which makes it possible for us to enter personally into the feelings, images, and concerns of the psalmists. Nevertheless, it is both useful and instructive to consult other good translations for comparative purposes.

I want to express my gratitude to a number of friends and to members of two congregations who have encouraged me to pursue the writing of this book and provided me with helpful comments on both the form and content of the meditations. I am especially appreciative of the support and help provided to me by Gordon Sorensen, Kathrine Laycock, and Hazelyn McComas. My wife, Edith, has been both a helpful critic and a patient proofreader. Finally, I want to acknowledge my deep gratitude to Sr. Elizabeth Sully, O.P., with whom I have shared a continuing quest for the vital balance between the prophetic and contemplative modes of spirituality. She continues to nourish my spirit in many ways.

Milwaukee
September 1990

Praying

Scripture

I lift up my hands to you in prayer;
like dry ground my soul is thirsty for you.
PSALM 143:6

Many readers will already be familiar with the practice of centering prayer and praying scripture. If so, a quick review of this section will be sufficient. For those who have not yet experienced this method of Christian prayer, it may be helpful to spend some time learning about it.

The term *praying scripture* is a contemporary name for a particular practice of prayer which has been a part of Christian spirituality since the time of the early church. In monastic spirituality it has long been known by its Latin name, *lectio divina,* or divine reading. As *lectio* is practiced in the monastic tradition, it includes both centering prayer and praying scripture.

Centering Prayer

The term *centering prayer* has come into common usage in recent years largely through the work of M. Basil Pennington. When understood in the larger context of *lectio,* it is helpful to distinguish between centering and praying scripture. Simply put, centering prayer can be thought of as the clearing of the mind of extraneous thoughts as a means of preparation for praying the scriptures. Praying scripture is the use of a brief passage of scripture as the basis for a period of prayer or meditation. First, a word about centering.

In his excellent book, A *Testament of Devotion*, the Quaker mystic, Thomas R. Kelly, says, "Deep within us all there is an amazing inner sanctuary of the soul, a holy place, a Divine Center, a speaking Voice, to which we may continuously return."[3] Centering prayer is a means by which we can get in touch with that "Divine Center" within us and thus enhance the experience of prayer, with or without the use of scripture.

Centering techniques are often recommended in stress workshops or other nonreligious settings simply as methods of relaxation. Centering prayer goes another step by adding an intentional spiritual focus to such techniques. As such, centering is done not simply out of a need to relax but as a conscious way of preparing oneself for prayer.

While we often offer brief prayers in the midst of other activities, centering prayer is a recognition of our need to enter into a sustained time of prayer to which we give our complete attention without trying to do something else at the same time. Thus, it requires the preparation of spirit, mind, and body.

Lawrence LeShan in *How to Meditate* puts his finger on the need for centering when he says that "if our bodies were half as unresponsive to our will as our minds are, we would never get across the street alive."[4] A simple five-minute experiment is enough to convince almost anyone of the truth of that statement. Try to sit for five minutes in a quiet room without thinking about anything. Or try to sit for five minutes and think of only *one* thing. How busy our brains are! We are always engaged in the process of taking in new data, reflecting on it, and filing it away in our memories. In the brief space of five minutes we may think about a dozen or more related and unrelated things. Again, LeShan says it well: "We find ourselves thinking of all sorts of other things rather than the simple thing we have just decided to think about" (p. 14). When the thoughts of a cook are often interrupted, the result may be something less than a culinary delight! When a student takes an examination in mathematics with a wandering mind, the grade may well be less than satisfactory. No wonder our experiences of prayer often seem to be sidetracked by other thoughts.

Simply put, centering is a practice by which we discipline our minds to think for a time about *one* thing rather than *many* things. This is done by concentrating on a single thing, while gently letting go of all other thoughts. For some the one thing may be an object such as a candle or an icon. Others focus on a word or a biblical phrase. The one thing can be anything you are comfortable with, such as the constant sound of a ticking clock or of water running through a radiator in the room where you are sitting. Focusing on one thing is *not* prayer. Rather it is a means of getting one's mind and spirit *ready* to pray.

Centering: The Technique

One popular means of centering is to sit quietly and try to think of nothing except counting your breaths as you exhale. Simply count "one" as you exhale the first breath, "two" as you exhale for the second time, and so forth. When you come to the fourth breath, begin counting again with "one": "One . . . two . . . three . . . four; one . . . two . . . three . . . four; one . . . two . . . three . . . four" becomes a pattern. Counting to higher numbers becomes a distraction in itself. Count only up to four and then begin over again.

After a very short time, you will undoubtedly have the experience of being distracted by other thoughts or you will find yourself counting beyond four. Don't despair. It happens to all of us, even to those who have been centering for a long time. When you become aware of the distraction, just let it go very gently. Say to yourself, "That is not why I'm here just now, I can come back to it later"; then return to your breath counting. This will happen repeatedly. Accept it as something normal, which it is, and continue the discipline of counting your breaths.

It will take time, perhaps several weeks, before you begin to gain some measure of discipline over your wandering mind. Don't let it worry you. It is simply part of being human. For most of us the thoughts which interrupt our attempts to become centered may be things we are worried about, things we need to accomplish during the day, or thoughts about something we did recently. If you are hungry, the interrupting thoughts may be of food.

If you find it difficult to dismiss such extraneous thoughts, you might find it helpful to imagine that you are setting beside a gently burning campfire. As thoughts come to mind, simply let them rise up and out of your vision with the smoke rising from the fire. Or imagine yourself sitting in the sand on the bottom of a lake surrounded by the gentle motion of plants in the water. Let your interrupting thoughts disappear from your sight like air bubbles rising to the surface of the lake.

For most people posture is an important part of centering. Sit erect in a comfortable, but fairly straight chair with both feet resting firmly on the floor. Let your hands relax in your lap. Hold your head in a balanced position so that it will not bob forward or sideways as you relax.

Begin by consciously relaxing the muscles in various parts of your body, starting with your feet and moving upward to the legs, hips, back, neck, arms, and finally the muscles in your face. Most of us tend to carry tension in our faces with tightened muscles in the forehead and around the mouth. Let them all relax.

Then take three or four slow, *deep* breaths. Hold the breath in your lungs a few seconds and then let it out slowly, breathing out the remaining tension in your body. Then, with your body relaxed, begin counting your breaths up to four, over and over, letting go of all extraneous thoughts. Continue for fifteen minutes or more until you feel centered.

The psalm meditations in this book each begin with a suggested Preparation that will help you to become centered. Those in the earlier psalms are especially directed toward the process of centering. The Preparation suggested in later psalm meditations will relate more directly to the content of the psalm itself. Remember that centering is worthwhile of itself. It is a wonderful means of relaxation. It is a good way to release tension in your body as well as in your mind. It may even be considered prayerful because it helps us to get in touch with our Divine Center where we can experience the presence of God in the joy of contemplative silence. It you have already learned how to center yourself, it is probably best to continue in your own accustomed way.

Praying Scripture

Centering is a way of preparing ourselves for the experience of praying the scriptures. Once you have centered, open your eyes and read a brief passage of scripture which you have selected in advance. Read it *slowly* and reflectively. Then be silent for a moment, taking time to find your center again if necessary. Then read the scripture a second time, taking time to linger over any phrase or thought which strikes you.

Most people find themselves particularly attracted to some phrase or verse during the second reading. It is not necessary to say to yourself, I need to look for a thought I like in this. If you are centered and open, the thought or phrase will likely lift itself up to you. It may strike you because it speaks to a need in you at the present time. Or it may be a beautiful metaphor or a new way of understanding an old idea. Whatever it is, come back to it after you have finished the reading for the second time.

Repeat that phrase or thought a few times. Let your mind play with it. Reflect on it. Ask yourself, why this particular thought? What might it be saying to me? How might this insight be incorporated into my own life? How does it relate to things that are happening in my life right now?

In the psalm meditations found in this book, a phrase or thought has already been chosen from the psalm to use as the focus of the meditation. This has been done intentionally to help those who are praying the scriptures for the first time to develop a sense of how the experience flows from centering to reading the psalm to reflecting on the theme or phrase and finally, to the incorporation of that idea in your own informal prayer. You may want to pray all of the psalms using the suggested themes. Or if you feel comfortable, you may wish to simply read the psalm from your Bible and trust the process to lift out a phrase or thought that strikes you personally. In either case, take time to reflect on the thought, play with it, ask questions related to it, and otherwise search out its relationship to who and where you are at this point in your life.

After you have reflected on the phrase or thought for a few moments and have a sense of having completed that phase of your prayer, move on to offer your own prayer to God in whatever style feels comfortable to you. You may want to share with God your insights and learnings from your reading and reflection. You may want to ask God to help you with a particular situation in your life. You may want to ask God for greater understanding or clarity about something.

Take time for your prayer. Allow yourself to listen to what God might be saying to you as well as what you are saying to God. Then, try to choose some *achievable* goal related to the prayer experience and ask God to help you to accomplish that goal in your life.

Finally, you will find that the discipline of praying scripture is enhanced if you take a moment to record four simple things in a prayer journal:

1) the date;
2) the scripture passage used;

3) the particular phrase or verse which struck you;

4) your insight or feeling which resulted from this prayer experience.

Such a record is not time consuming and will become more and more valuable after several months or years of praying scripture. It will provide a ready source of valuable information about your spiritual growth, which may otherwise be lost in the process.

The
Language of
the Psalms

*How can we sing the Lord's song in a foreign
land?*

PSALM 137:4 [NRSV]

I t is important to approach the Psalms with some understanding of
the multitude of themes they address and an awareness of their
corporate and individual use (see Appendix A, "Types of Psalms"). It is
also essential to come to them with a sensitivity to the problems of
language. The Psalms are a specialized type of literature from a culture
vastly different in time and place from our own. We are also reading
them in translation from a language which differs greatly from our own.

The problems of translation alone are overwhelming. The Psalms
were originally written in Hebrew, a language that is not always easily
translated into English. There are many Hebrew words for which there
simply is no adequate English equivalent. The word *hesed* is a good
example. It is translated variously, "steadfast love" (RSV), "constant
love" (TEV), and "kindness" (NAB). There are other versions which
vary the translation from verse to verse. The KJV uses "lovingkindness,"
"mercy," and "goodness" while the NEB uses "unfailing love," "constant

love," and "true love." Yet, none of these translations, individually or collectively, adequately conveys the rich meaning of the original Hebrew word.

Cultural Differences

Other language problems arise from cultural differences. The English language, because of our history and culture, has become relatively precise and scientific compared to the more poetic or metaphorical use of language in the East and the Middle East. Other differences result from the fact that those who wrote the original biblical language were agrarian or nomadic, unlike most of us who read their words many centuries later. The Bible often uses imagery of sheep and shepherds, yet many in our own time have never seen a sheep except perhaps on television!

Other factors like geography, geology, and climate also influence language. Those who have visited Israel and have noticed the presence of stone almost everywhere in the land are sensitive to the many references to stones in the gospels. Because water was relatively scarce in the land of our biblical ancestors they used it and wrote about it in ways that we who have abundant water do not always appreciate. Likewise, the rapid pace of life in our highly mobile world means that our concept of time is different than that of our spiritual ancestors, who lived by the sun and needed proportionately larger amounts of time simply to get from place to place. When we begin to appreciate the culture of those who wrote the psalms, we gain new insights into their use of language.

Precise Language and Poetic Language

Walter Brueggemann in *Praying the Psalms*, speaks of the "liberation of language."[5] He says that in our own time the function of language is primarily

> to report and describe what already exists. The usefulness of such language is obvious. It lets us be precise and unambiguous. It even lets us control. But it is one-dimensional language that must necessarily be without passion and without eloquence and indeed without boldness. . . . Such language is useful for managing

things. But it makes no impact on how things really are, for things would be the same even if there were no such speech.

(p. 28)

On the other hand, Brueggemann says, the language of the Psalms

does not *describe* what is. It *evokes* to being what is not until it has been spoken. This kind of speech resists discipline, shuns precision, delights in ambiguity, is profoundly creative, and is itself an exercise in freedom. In using speech in this way, we are in fact doing in a derivative way what God has done in the creation narratives of Genesis. We are calling into being that which does not yet exist.

(p. 28)

It is extremely difficult to grasp the full meaning of the Psalms, much less to pray them, without some understanding of the difference between the way the psalmists used language and the way we use it.

Thus, when we read or pray the Psalms, it is necessary to temporarily abandon the assumptions which we take for granted about our own use of language. Only then can we enter into the world of language as it is used in the Psalms, and indeed in much of the Bible. Psalm 131 is one of the shortest psalms of the entire Psalter. It serves well to illustrate the language of the Psalms.

> *Lord, I have given up my pride*
> *and turned away from my arrogance.*
> *I am not concerned with great matters*
> *or with subjects too difficult for me.*
> *Instead, I am content and at peace.*
> *As a child lies quietly in its mother's arms,*
> *so my heart is quiet within me.*
> *Israel, trust in the Lord now and forever!*

Enemies, Pits, Wings, and Idols

Another language problem has to do with words used frequently in the Psalms which, for various reasons, may cause difficulty for the

[29]

modern reader. The problem is easily overcome if we are aware of those words and grant ourselves permission to bring their meaning up to date for our own usage. Let us look briefly at four words: *enemies, pits, wings,* and *idols.*

In the Today's English Version of the Psalms, the word *enemies* occurs over 160 times and in 70 different psalms. Moreover it is often used in a context which implies anger, vengeance, or even paranoia on the part of the psalmist. Most often the enemy or enemies are not identified. The frequency with which the word is used and the way it is used leave us considerable room for interpretation. It may well be that the original Hebrew word does not carry the same heavy emotional feeling that we associate with our word enemy.

It is important to remember that there are cultural and theological differences between the original intent of the word and our reading of it in a very different time and place. It is also important to remember that we who read and pray the Psalms today are different people with different life experiences. Thus we need to give ourselves permission to translate such terms into concepts which are meaningful in our own lives.

Several years ago I prayed through the Psalms over a period of several months. One day I came to Psalm 109 and, after centering, began to read the psalm for the first time. As I came near to the final verses, I thought, Good heavens, how can I pray this? There is nothing here but anger and vengeance. Fortunately, I had learned by this time to be faithful to the process. After a moment of quiet, I began reading through the psalm a second time. But again, I thought, What is there of redeeming value in this psalm? Then, suddenly, I was struck with the realization that I carried within me that very day the same feelings of anger toward a co-worker who was in the next room! I suddenly realized that I was every bit as angry as the psalmist. As I prayed the psalm I was confronted with the necessity of owning the anger within me. Once I had done that, the next step was to search for the seeds of something redemptive in the brokenness of that relationship.

A few days later I was confronted with the word *enemies* in another psalm. This time my reflection revealed to me that I was angry at several persons on a committee which a few days earlier had rejected one of my ideas that I felt strongly about. I discovered that I had been grumbling to myself about these people to the point of thinking of them as enemies! Praying the psalm revealed to me that they were *not* my enemies, but simply friends who didn't have an appreciation of something about which I felt so deeply. The real insight was that the human condition causes us to turn those who simply misunderstand or disagree with us into enemies. Now, when I come across the word *enemies* in a psalm, I stop to ask myself, who are the people or conditions in my life right now whom I have turned into enemies and what do I need to do to change that situation?

The word *pit* occurs in several of the psalms, almost always associated with *enemies:*

> *I waited patiently for the Lord's help;*
> * then he listened to me and heard my cry.*
> *He pulled me out of a dangerous pit,*
> * out of the deadly quicksand.*
> *He set me safely on a rock and made me secure.*   (40:1-2)

> *My enemies have spread a net to catch me;*
> * I am overcome with distress.*
> *They dug a pit in my path,*
> * but fell into it themselves.*   (57:6)

> *Proud men, who do not obey your law,*
> * have dug pits to trap me.*   (119:85)

Our tendency to use language precisely is such that we are quick to conjure up images of literal pits dug in the path so that someone will fall into them and be trapped. And for some like Joseph (Gen. 37:21-28) and Jeremiah (Jer. 38:1-13), the experience of being in the pit was quite literal! But, it is also used as a metaphor. Even in our own language we say things like, "Life is really the pits for me right now" or "He got the cherries and she got the pits." As we read the Psalms, we need to allow ourselves space to play with such images until we can relate them to our own situation. Some days life *is* the pits!

Another image used in several of the psalms is that of God's "wings":

> *How precious, O God, is your constant love!*
> *We find protection under the shadow of your wings.*   (36:7)

> *He will cover you with his wings;*
> *you will be safe in his care;*
> *his faithfulness will protect and defend you.* (91:4)

It is possible that the phrase "in the shadow of your wings" may be a reference to the winged creatures which stood in the Temple (1 Kings 6:23-28). Isaiah speaks of the "flaming creatures," each of which had six wings, when he tells of his call in the Temple (Isaiah 6:1-4). But, there are also metaphorical references to the wings of God:

> *You saw what I, the Lord, did to the Egyptians and how I carried you as an eagle carries her young on her wings, and brought you here to me.* (Exod. 19:4)

> *Jerusalem, Jerusalem! You kill the prophets, you stone the messengers God has sent you! How many times I wanted to put my arms around all your people, just as a hen gathers her chicks under her wings, but you would not let me!* (Luke 13:34)

Finally, let us look at one more image used in the Psalms, that of "idols":

> *Who has the right to go up the Lord's hill?*
> *Who may enter his holy Temple?*
> *Those who are pure in act and in thought,*
>   *who do not worship idols or make false promises.* (24:3-4)

> *Happy are those who trust the Lord,*
> *who do not turn to idols*
>   *or join those who worship false gods.* (40:4)

> *Why should the nations ask us,*
>   *"Where is your God?"*
> *Our God is in heaven;*
>   *he does whatever he wishes.*
> *Their gods are made of silver and gold,*
>   *formed by human hands.*
> *They have mouths, but cannot speak,*
>   *and eyes, but cannot see.*
> *They have ears, but cannot hear,*

and noses, but cannot smell.
They have hands, but cannot feel,
    and feet, but cannot walk;
    they cannot make a sound.
May all who made them and who trust in them
    become like the idols they have made.   (115:2-8)

Surely it is not difficult for us to make the transition between the idols made of gold and silver in the Psalms and the idols of our own culture. We are surrounded by billboards, TV commercials, and newspaper ads urging us to worship all kinds of idols!

Translations of the Bible

No discussion of the language of the Psalms would be complete without mention of the language of different translations of the Bible. Many of our grandparents knew only the Authorized or King James Version (KJV) of the Bible. Its use of Elizabethan English sets it apart from most modern translations. It is not the language that we use in our everyday conversations. Many of the words used in the KJV have changed in meaning since it was first published in the seventeenth century. In addition, modern biblical scholarship, together with the discovery of earlier manuscripts of many biblical books, has caused the KJV to be out of date both in terms of accuracy and of translation.

Fortunately, we live in a time when there are many good translations of the Bible available. Opinions differ as to which is best. From the point of view of biblical scholarship, the New Revised Standard Version is probably the single most *accurate* translation of the Bible available to us today. The New English Bible, the New Jerusalem Bible, the Today's English Version, and the New American Bible are also acceptable, and among these, the choice is largely a matter of personal preference. Even so, it is best not to limit one's reading to any one translation simply out of habit or convenience. A comparison of several translations will often provide fresh insight into a given text. This is certainly true of the Psalms. Those who want to pray the scriptures might be well advised to avoid *paraphrased* versions of the Bible which have a tendency to sacrifice accuracy in favor of contemporary language.

Almost all the biblical references used in this book, including the phrases used as titles for the psalm meditations, are from the Today's English Version (TEV). The TEV, also known as the *Good News Bible*, is highly respected for its accurate rendering of the original texts into clear and contemporary English. The TEV also breaks the text up into natural sections with subheadings for easy reference. Those who begin to pray the psalms using the meditations offered in this book will find it especially helpful to use the TEV for the readings. Nevertheless, it is often helpful to compare the language of a particular text with that in other good translations. Later you may wish to read or pray the Psalms again using another translation.

Inclusive Language

Finally, a note about inclusive language. While there are still some who insist that they are comfortable with the more traditional masculine language of the Bible, the movement is clearly in the direction of inclusiveness. I am personally committed to the use of inclusive language in my writing and preaching, and whenever possible in the public reading of scripture. In writing the material used in the psalm meditations in the book, I have sought to eliminate unnecessary masculine language in biblical quotations by editing phrases or by paraphrasing. In some instances I have replaced masculine pronouns with a gender-neutral word, indicating the change by placing the new word in brackets. Whenever possible, I have used the same methods with respect to masculine pronouns referring to God.

Praying with

Our Spiritual

Ancestors

Think of the rock from which you came,
the quarry from which you were cut.
Think of your ancestor, Abraham,
and of Sarah, from whom you are descended.

ISAIAH 51:1-2

The Book of Psalms has always occupied a place of special honor among Christians. The Psalms are often quoted in the Christian scriptures. Since the time of the early church, the Psalms have been incorporated into Christian worship and have also played an important role in individual Christian piety. How many Christians have had their own pocket edition of the "New Testament with Psalms"!

Nevertheless, it is vitally important to remember that the Psalms are a product of the Jewish faith and that their content and style are thoroughly Jewish. The church, uneasy with its own Jewish roots, has long struggled with its relationship to the Hebrew scriptures. Since the time of Marcion, who put forth the view that Christianity had superseded Judaism and therefore was superior to it, the church has often had a tendency to "Christianize" the Psalms along with other parts of the Hebrew scriptures, particularly the prophets. This has been done by picking and choosing those parts of the Hebrew scriptures which will be remembered, quoted, and used in the liturgy of the church, and also by lifting parts of the scriptures out of context in order to provide a

[35]

historical backdrop compatible with cherished Christian beliefs. Our continuing use of the term *Old Testament* when referring to the Hebrew scriptures may be an unconscious continuation of the heresy of Marcion. Those who want to be serious in their reading and praying of the Psalms need to be sensitive to the historical and theological integrity of the Hebrew scriptures.

Thoughtful Christians need to seek a fuller understanding of the Jewish roots of the Christian Church. (For a challenging discussion of the relationship between Judaism and Christianity, see Chapter 4 of Walter Brueggeman's *Praying the Psalms*.) Among other things we must remember that Jesus himself prayed and quoted the Psalms *as a Jew*.

I have long been fond of the story of God's covenant with Abram as it is found in Genesis. Abram and Sarai were old and Sarai was childless. In a vision Abram was taken outside his tent by God to look at the magnificent canopy of stars in the sky. The Lord said to Abram, "Look at the sky and try to count the stars; you will have as many descendants as that" (Gen.15:5). God was faithful to the covenant, and today Abraham is the common spiritual ancestor of Jews, Christians, and Moslems!

For Christians who want to approach the Hebrew scriptures with both reverence and integrity, this is a place to begin. Abraham and Sarah are *our* ancestors too! While we may not be Jews, we need to claim that Judaism is a vital part of our own spiritual tradition. To take seriously our relationship to the Hebrew scriptures is to walk in fragile territory. But to do so with humility and openness enables us to walk with our common spiritual ancestor, Moses, on holy ground. The Psalms are filled with stories, traditions, and references to a rich heritage, which is shared by Jews and Christians alike.

> *Our ancestors put their trust in you;*
> *they trusted you, and you saved them.*
> *They called to you and escaped from danger;*
> *they trusted you and were not disappointed.*
> (22:4-5)

> *Hear my prayer, Lord, and listen to my cry;*
> *come to my aid when I weep.*
> *Like all my ancestors*
> *I am only your guest for a little while.*
> (39:12)

With our own ears we have heard it, O God—
  our ancestors have told us about it,
  about the great things you did in their time,
  in the days of long ago.

(44:1)

[God] changed the sea into dry land;
  our ancestors crossed the river on foot.
There we rejoiced because of what [God] did.

(66:6)

[God] gave laws to the people of Israel
  and commandments to the descendants of Jacob.
[God] instructed our ancestors
  to teach [God's] laws to their children.
In this way they also will put their trust in
  God and not forget what [God] has done,
but always obey [God's] commandments.

(78:5,7)

Listen today to what [God] says: "Don't be
  stubborn, as your ancestors were at Meribah,
  as they were that day in the desert at Massah.
There they put me to the test and tried me,
  although they had seen what I did for them.

(95:7b-9)

We have sinned as our ancestors did;
  we have been wicked and evil.
Our ancestors in Egypt did not understand God's
  wonderful acts;
they forgot the many times [God] showed them
  [God's] love, and they rebelled against the Al-
  mighty at the Red Sea.

(106:6-7)

Suggestions for Using the Meditations

Your word is a lamp to guide me and a light for my path.

T he psalm meditations offered in this book are intended to serve as an introduction to praying scripture, with selected psalms serving as the immediate vehicle. Most of the Psalms were originally used either as individual or community prayers and are easily adapted for use as prayers in our own time. There are, however, a few psalms which for one reason or another do not lend themselves to being prayed. Psalm 45, for example, is not a prayer at all, but a song composed for a royal wedding. While attempts have been made to allegorize its meaning, it remains a problem from the point of view of prayer. This is not to say that this or a similar psalm cannot be used in our prayers. It is just that they may be more difficult to pray. Thus this book contains 150 meditations based on 128 of the Psalms.

In each psalm or portion of a psalm a phrase has been chosen to lift up a major theme for prayer. In addition to the major theme, most meditations also address additional themes in one way or another. An index of themes has been included (Appendix C) to assist those who may wish to pursue a particular theme in other psalms or simply to locate a meditation which speaks to a theme of special interest to the reader. The format of each meditation is as follows:

[39]

Introduction: Information is provided concerning the origin, structure, and use of the psalm by individuals or by a community of worshipers in the Temple, in order to make the psalm as understandable as possible as we begin to pray it.

Preparation: This section makes suggestions for getting ready to pray the psalm in the context of centering prayer.

Reading: In most cases it will be suggested that the psalm be read at least twice, slowly and reflectively.

Reflection: Suggested questions and observations are provided to stimulate personal reflection and meditation on the psalm.

Prayer: Following a period of reflection, a possible approach to prayer is offered, related to the theme of the psalm.

Preparation

The Preparation suggestions have been designed to be helpful to those who have had little or no experience with centering prayer. The earlier meditations emphasize learning how to become centered in order to be more relaxed and focused in the actual experience of praying the psalm. Those who have already had experience with centering prayer and feel comfortable with it should feel free to continue using their own way of centering. For those with little or no experience a few reminders may be helpful:

1. Begin with a moment or two of gentle exercise.
2. Sit with your back straight, feet on the floor, head balanced.
3. Consciously relax all muscles in the body, including facial muscles.
4. Take three or four long, slow, deep breaths.
5. Begin counting your breaths up to four.
6. Allow extraneous thoughts to drift away.
7. When you feel you are ready, begin reading the psalm.

Reading

The importance of reading the psalms *slowly* and *reflectively* cannot be stressed too much. Most of us are taught to read at a fairly rapid pace, both silently and aloud. Scripture is not scientific or factual data to be rushed through in order to gain a general impression of its content. Nor should it be approached with the thought of getting to the point at the end. When we pray scripture, God may be asking us to wrestle with an idea which occurs at any point in the selected passage. Thus every phrase is important, every word a potential source of new challenge and insight. Take plenty of time to read the passage very slowly, lingering over whatever intrigues you, savoring images, and reflecting on new ideas. Take a moment or two to relax after you have read it for the first time. Then go back and read it a second time, even more slowly, paying attention to any phrase which seems to address you.

Reflection

After you have read the psalm a second time, relax, continue in your centering, and let your mind *play* with the ideas, words, and thoughts which have emerged as you read. Ask yourself, what is this phrase saying to *me*? Why did I react to it the way I did? How does this theme relate to my own experience? Make use of the suggested reflections on the theme of the psalm if they are helpful. If not, reflect on your own ideas and reactions. Ask yourself how you *feel* about this psalm or about some of the specific phrases in it. Allow several minutes for this reflection process. You will know when you have finished and are ready to move on to your prayer.

Prayer

When you are ready to pray (although you have been praying all along as you centered, read, and reflected on the scripture), take time for a more structured prayer with God according to your personal pattern and experience. Your prayer may take the form of a dialogue between you and God. You may want to share your feelings with God. You may simply want to listen to God in the silence. Ask God to help you to continue reflecting and learning from the psalm throughout the day. Ask for support as you try to change or improve something in your life, start a new discipline, or simply be more prayerful.

When your prayer is completed, bring your experience to a close by using a favorite line of scripture, the Lord's Prayer, or anything else that might be meaningful to you. You may wish to choose something that will become a personal ritual for you as you continue to pray the psalms each day. After you have finished, give yourself time to readjust to the tasks, demands, and opportunities of the day.

And now, a word about the phrases which have been chosen as titles for the psalm meditations. Each has been chosen partly to illustrate the rich imagery of the psalms, but also as a beginning focus on a theme that will be carried through the reading, reflection, and prayer suggestions for the particular psalm. Obviously you will find that some of these suggested themes will be meaningful and helpful, while others will be less helpful. After you have had some experience praying the scriptures, you will no longer need a suggested theme. Your theme will emerge naturally as you read and pray any passage of scripture. Your theme is the word, phrase, or thought which begins to intrigue you as you read it. When something deep inside you recognizes that you are being spoken to out of the scripture, it is a bit like an "a-ha" moment. Don't force it by consciously looking for an insight. Rather, allow it to look for you.

Perhaps it goes without saying that when we have prayed a psalm or any other passage of scripture once, we have not exhausted what it may have to say to us. We will be able to come back to it several months or years later and discover that we are addressed by a different idea or phrase because we are coming to it from a different place in life. It may also be helpful to read it later in another translation, since different words speak to each of us in different ways.

The psalm meditations in this book, written primarily for private use by individuals, are readily adaptable for use in small groups. The format, designed to help individuals learn to pray the scriptures by doing it, will also be helpful for groups of persons seeking to learn together. Experienced leaders will have used a similar format to conduct guided meditations and will find the questions and other suggestions in the Reflection section of each meditation useful in helping those new to *lectio* to move from an academic approach to scripture study to a more affective format. Those learning to pray the scriptures in group settings should be encouraged, for example, to take time to discover the emotional content of various psalms or to put themselves in the place of the author of a particular psalm, once they have a working understanding of the circumstances and conditions reflected in the psalm.

Like
Trees
That
Grow
Beside
a Stream

Psalm 1

"Like trees that grow beside a stream"

Introduction: This psalm was intentionally placed at the beginning of the Psalter as a kind of preface. It was intended to be an announcement of joy for all who continuously return to the psalms for meditation. Those who study God's law will be "like trees that grow beside a stream."

Preparation: Find a quiet time and place where you will not be interrupted. Close your eyes and relax. Let go of all the thoughts which clutter your mind; then imagine that you are sitting beside a gentle stream . . . listen to the water.

Read Psalm 1: Read the psalm slowly. Pause and be quiet for a moment; then read it again, slowly.

Reflection: What would it be like for you to have a quiet place where you could go regularly to slow down for a few minutes to experience God's peace?

How do you feel about the image of our being like "trees that grow beside a stream"? How does that image relate to the theme of God's constant guidance and protection?

Prayer: Share your reflections with God. Be quiet a moment. Give thanks for all that God does to guide and protect you even when you don't know it.

Psalm 2

"Why do the nations plan rebellion?"

Introduction: This is one of the "royal psalms" associated with a king of Israel. It is an affirmation that the recently anointed king is the regent of the Lord. Surrounding nations may be moving against the new king, but God mocks them (verses 4-6). The Lord speaks to the king in verses 7-9, while verses 10-12 are a warning for other kings to cease their rebellion.

Preparation: As you prepare to pray this psalm, sit quietly for a moment or two. Then consciously relax various groups of muscles in your body, beginning with your feet and moving upward. Don't forget to let go of the tension in your jaws, lips, and eyes.

Read Psalm 2: Read the psalm slowly, watching for the themes outlined in the introduction above. Then read it again, allowing it to speak to you.

Reflection: It has been said that nations behave very much the same way that individuals behave, arguing about who is the most important, etc. How much of such national behavior is a waste of energy which might have gone into a more constructive relationship?

Prayer: Offer your prayer for the nations and leaders of the world, that we might learn how to be more cooperative and trusting.

Psalm 3

"They talk about me"

Introduction: This is a personal psalm in which the author struggles, as we all do, with the tension between faith and fear. The psalms often speak of "enemies," which may sound strange to us. Yet, we often have similar feelings about others, although we may not refer to them as enemies.

Preparation: Sit quietly for a moment; then take several long, slow, deep breaths, allowing the tension to leave your body as you exhale. Breathe in peace.

Read Psalm 3: Read the psalm slowly and reflectively. Then after a moment of silence, read it again, slowly.

Reflection: Who or what are the "enemies" in your life right now? Do you sometimes promote someone to the status of enemy just because he or she sees things differently than you do, or perhaps misunderstands you? Is such a person really an enemy? What might be a better way to relate to such a person?

Prayer: Ask God to help you with your enemy problem. Ask for the patience and love to change enemies into friends. Pray for those you may sometimes think of as enemies.

Psalm 4

"How long will you love what is worthless?"

Introduction:	This lament is a prayer of deep confidence and trust in God by someone who seems to be surrounded by those who have false or misplaced values. While the difficulties seem to press in from all sides, the psalm suggests that real peace of mind is found by those who trust in God. The joy received from God is valued more than material things sought by others.
Preparation:	Take a few minutes to make a mental listing of the "things" in your life . . . and what importance you attach to them. Then sit quietly for several minutes and let them go. Open yourself to receive God's blessing of joy.
Read Psalm 4:	Read the psalm slowly, taking time to note the request made in verse 1; the "lecture" to others in verses 2-5; and the thanksgiving to God in verses 6-8.
Reflection:	How much do you value material things? What do you *really* value? What might it mean for you to "offer the right sacrifices" to God? When you go to bed at night, do you sleep in peace? or are you troubled with the things which concern you during the day? How many of those things are worth losing sleep over?
Prayer:	Let your prayer flow out of your reflections. Ask God to help you discover what needs to change in your life, so that you will not "love what is worthless."

Psalm 5

"All who find safety in you will rejoice"

Introduction: As in a number of the psalms, the author here is beset by enemies who are deceitful, flattering, and not to be trusted. The lack of specific details enables the psalm to be prayed by anyone. We can imagine the psalmist praying these words while walking to the Temple for the morning sacrifice. It is both a prayer and a meditation which contrasts those who are righteous with those who are evil. The psalmist prays to be led to do God's will and asks that God's way might be made plain.

Preparation: As you settle into a quiet, prayerful place, take time to breathe deeply and relax your body. Release all those things on your mind's agenda, so that you will be free to give your complete attention to reading and praying the psalm.

Read Psalm 5: Read the psalm slowly to get a sense of its content and flow. Then after a moment or two of silence, read it again even more slowly, imagining yourself praying it as you walk to your place of worship early in the morning.

Reflection: Is there someone you know who "can never be trusted" or whose words are "flattering and smooth, but full of deadly deceit"?

Prayer: Can you offer your prayer to God without feeling self-righteous about yourself as compared to your enemies?

Psalm 6

"My pillow is soaked with tears"

Introduction: Psalm 6 is the first of the penitential psalms: 6, 32, 38, 51, 102, 130, and 143. The psalmist is burdened both by sin and with its consequences. The feelings of the psalmist sound very much like the symptoms of what we now call depression. Thus the prayer pleads for forgiveness, not only for the past sin, but also for the present consequences of that sin, including harsh or cruel treatment by friends. The last verses reflect the confidence of the psalmist that God *will* hear the prayer and that forgiveness *will* come.

Preparation: Prepare for yourself a comfortable, quiet place, free from interruptions and distractions. Give yourself plenty of time to let go of all the thoughts and concerns that fill your mind. Take several long, slow, deep breaths.

Read Psalm 6: Read the psalm slowly and thoughtfully. After two or three minutes, read it a second time.

Reflection: Do you remember a time when you felt depressed about a personal problem and withdrew from your friends? Can you identify with any of the feelings of the psalmist? Which feelings?

Prayer: Give thanks to God who is present to us even when we feel alone and miserable. Share your own feelings with God.

Psalm 7

"Rescue me and save me from all who pursue me"

Introduction: Psalm 7 is the prayer of one who has been unjustly accused. The psalmist has come to the Temple to appeal in person to the God of justice. Verses 3-5 offer a brutal self-examination after which God is asked to declare the psalmist innocent and find the accusers guilty. The point is made in verses 14-16 that those who plot evil end up caught in their own traps. The psalm ends on a note of praise and thanksgiving for God's justice.

Preparation: The psalmist in this case has come to the Temple where one could experience a sense of safety and fairness not found in the circumstances of life. We also need to find a place where we can pray in safety and peace, uninterrupted by ordinary things like work, the telephone, etc. Does your place of prayer feel like a place of safety and peace? Do you need to find a better place?

Read Psalm 7: Read Psalm 7 noting the various sections mentioned in the introduction. Pause a moment or two before reading it again.

Reflection: Do you ever feel "pursued" by anyone, such as your employer or others to whom you are accountable? Do you feel that others have unjust expectations of you? Examine yourself to see if you have contributed to the situation by your own actions or thoughts.

Prayer: Share with God any ways in which you feel pursued, acknowledging any responsibility you may have for the situation.

Psalm 8

"Your greatness is seen in all the world"

Introduction:	One could almost imagine this great hymn of praise being sung by the first human beings after God finished creating the heavens and the earth. It was probably used in the evening liturgy of the Temple with the identical first and last lines sung by the congregation, and the verses in between by a cantor.
Preparation:	It is difficult to imagine praying the psalm anywhere but outdoors in a place where one can experience the full glory of nature. Give yourself time to imagine such a setting. Breathe the fresh air; listen to the songs of birds; in your mind's eye, watch a full moon rise over your favorite landscape.
Read Psalm 8:	Read the psalm, pausing after each line, allowing yourself time to see each scene as it is described.
Reflection:	Where do *you* see the greatness of God in the world? How does "mere man" come to be appointed "ruler over everything" God made? Think about how the earth has changed under the stewardship of human beings. Have we increased or decreased the way God's greatness can be "seen in all the world"?
Prayer:	Allow your prayer to flow out of your reflections.

Psalm 9

"The Lord is a refuge for the oppressed"

Introduction:	Psalms 9 and 10 were originally a single alphabetical acrostic—each succeeding verse beginning with the next letter of the 22-letter Hebrew alphabet. The fact that Psalm 10 bears no Hebrew title is seen by scholars as further evidence that it was originally a continuation of Psalm 9. While the two psalms share common themes, the mood is somewhat different. Psalm 9 seems to be a thanksgiving to God for Jerusalem's having been delivered from military invasion, while Psalm 10 is a call for justice.
Preparation:	Is your time for prayer and meditation too hurried? Take a moment to evaluate how you feel about the *time* you spend praying. If you feel rushed, what can you do to overcome that feeling? Someone has said, "If you are too busy to pray, you are too busy."
Read Psalm 9:	Read the psalm slowly, pausing after verses 6, 12, and 14 to reflect briefly on the mood of each section.
Reflection:	In what ways is God "a refuge for the oppressed"? Does God help us turn our suffering into solitude and our solitude into an opportunity for insight, gentleness, and understanding?
Prayer:	Give thanks that all things *do* seem to work together for good. Is there some way that God can work through *you* to provide a refuge for the oppressed?

Psalm 10

"O Lord . . . remember those who are suffering!"

Introduction:	While Psalm 10 is technically a continuation of Psalm 9, the mood changes. It is a prayer for God to bring justice to the poor and oppressed. As such it contains an interesting reflection on the old question, "why do the wicked seem to prosper while the good suffer?" The apparent success of the wicked is a source of temptation to those who seek a life of righteousness. The psalm ends with the faithful assertion that God *will* hear the cries of the oppressed and judge in their behalf.
Preparation:	Have you experimented with different times of the day for your praying of the scriptures? Find the time which seems to work best for you. Let it be a time when you can feel free of pressures and anxieties. Give yourself permission to see your prayer time as valuable and important.
Read Psalm 10:	Read the psalm reflectively, noting the many *feelings* of the author. Pause. Read it again.
Reflection:	Why does the psalmist dwell so long on those who are "wicked"? Do the evil really act as if "God doesn't matter"? Do you ever act that way? Do you long to see your enemies punished? Would that really help? Would it be better if we left such judgments up to God?
Prayer:	Share with God your feelings about those who seem to you to be unjust or wicked. Pray for them as well as for their victims.

[54]

Psalm 11

"When everything falls apart"

Introduction: When a person is in danger, what could be more
natural than going into hiding? And in Israel, where
is there a better place to hide than in the mountains?
The author of this psalm was in danger, and the
opening verse implies that friends had offered the
advice, "head for the hills." But the psalmist rejects
the "foolish" advice, choosing instead to trust in God.
To run away would be to "give in" and might have the
effect of admitting moral failure to oneself, if not also
to others. So the decision is made to trust in the
justice and protection of God and to "live in his
presence."

Preparation: As you prepare to pray this psalm, know that you do
not have to go into hiding, but that you will find
peace in God's presence wherever you may be.

Read Psalm 11: Read the psalm first to become familiar with the
reasoning of the psalmist in the light of the introduction above. Then read it a second time, trying to feel
what the psalmist felt.

Reflection: Can you remember a time when you were accused of
something and were tempted to run away? How do you
feel about the psalmist's decision to trust in God,
rather than go into hiding?

Prayer: Ask God to grant you such faith that you will not be
tempted to flee "when everything falls apart."

Psalm 12

"Silence those flattering tongues"

Introduction: This is a psalm for liturgical use; it might be called a "liturgy of regrouping." Separate choral groups are heard in verses 2-3, 4, and 5. The final verses (7-8) restate the theme and offer a summary prayer for protection from those whose words are marked by insincerity and flattery.

Preparation: Find your personal quiet place; give yourself the time to relax and let go of other thoughts and pressures. Tune in to the quietness . . . let it fill your spirit with peace. Hold onto that peace . . . gently let go of any distractions.

Read Psalm 12: Take time to really hear what is meant.

Reflection: How do you feel when everyone around you seems to be speaking with "flattering words" designed more to impress others than to genuinely praise? Do you get tired of people who boast about themselves, their experiences, and their achievements? Do you find yourself using flattering words and boasting to impress others? Why? Does it really impress others?

Prayer: Ask God to make others (and yourself) more aware of such shallow words. Ask God to help you silence your "flattering tongue." Ask for the gift of learning how to offer sincere praise to others, when you expect nothing in return.

Psalm 13

"How much longer will you forget me, Lord?"

Introduction: Psalm 13 is a very personal prayer of one who is ill, perhaps terminally ill. Jewish tradition allows for the expression of both positive and negative feelings about God in prayer. Here the psalmist expresses frustration, impatience, and even anger. Just as we often feel better and have our perspective restored after "getting it off our chest," the psalm closes with a sense of faith and confidence in the constancy of God's love. The frustration of the present situation does not obscure the fact of God's care.

Preparation: Take a few deep breaths to release the tension in your body. Dismiss the many concerns and thoughts that flash through your mind; remind yourself that there will be time for them later.

Read Psalm 13: Read the psalm slowly. Be quiet for a moment; then read it again, as if YOU had written it.

Reflection: Do you sometimes have negative feelings about God? Ask yourself: Is God absent from me? Or, am I absent from God?

Prayer: Allow yourself to express feelings of anger, frustration, impatience, etc., even if they are directed toward God. It is OK to have such feelings and to share them! Give thanks to God for creating us as *feeling* persons. Give thanks for the freedom which comes when we have been honest about our feelings.

Psalm 15

"Whoever does these things . . . "

Introduction: This teaching psalm begins with a question, "Lord, who may enter your Temple?" This question was asked of visitors to the Temple, who could not be admitted until they recited answers similar to those in verses 2-5. Coming near to God was not just a matter of external ritual, but the living of a life that produced fruits. The reward is found in the final sentence: "Whoever does these things will always be secure."

Preparation: Close your eyes; imagine yourself on a pilgrimage to the Temple of the Lord. As you arrive at the gate of the Temple, you want your heart to be pure and your mind open to receive whatever spiritual truth might be given to you.

Read Psalm 15: Read the psalm slowly, taking time to reflect on each of the requirements for entering into the presence of God.

Reflection: How do you feel about the requirements for entering the Temple? Which requirements might pose a difficulty in your own life? What might you do in your own life to come closer to the standards set by these requirements?

Prayer: Let your prayer flow naturally out of the things you feel as a result of praying this psalm.

Psalm 16

"In the night my conscience warns me"

Introduction: This is a psalm of spiritual maturity. It is filled with thankfulness, confidence, and wisdom. One wants to meet the "saint" who first offered this prayer. We long to achieve such a mature relationship with God.

Preparation: Sit quietly. One by one, strip away the layers of anxiety and concern that grip you in so much of your daily life. You can return to them later, if need be. For now, let them go with a series of deep breaths. Breathe in calmness, exhale distractions.

Read Psalm 16: Pause at the end of each verse to reflect on its richness. Read the psalm a second time, savoring the absolute confidence in God's goodness.

Reflection: Can you thank God for "all the good things" you have? What is the meaning of "you give me all I need"? How do your dreams serve to integrate all that happens in your daily life? Is God present, even in your dreaming, to make you more whole? Does God "warn" you in the night? Is it possible that your spirit continues in prayer throughout the night?

Prayer: In humility be thankful for all that God provides for you. What more could you ask for? Offer praise for God's continuing care in the night when you "rest in the Lord."

Psalm 17

"You will judge in my favor, because you know what is right"

Introduction: Psalm 17 is another prayer for a just judgment on the part of one who has been righteous but is still the target of those who "have no pity." The psalmist may have taken refuge in the Temple while waiting for vindication of innocence. There is a call for the punishment of surrounding enemies even to the third generation. The psalm begins with confidence in God's judgment and ends in confidence that God's presence is assured.

Preparation: In opening ourselves to the presence of God in prayer, we lay aside all other thoughts, entering into a state of consciousness that is different than our usual mode of being, but no less normal. Allow yourself to let go of the clutter of your mind in order to be open to God's presence.

Read Psalm 17: Read the psalm, allowing yourself to enter into the mind and heart of the psalmist. Read it again simply to feel what the psalmist feels, without making any value judgments of your own.

Reflection: Can you feel what the psalmist must have felt? What is the difference between the confidence in one's own righteousness found in verses 3-4 and a genuine sense of humility? How do you feel about the psalmist's call for the punishment of enemies in verses 13-14?

Prayer: Ask for the grace to trust your life to God's care in all circumstances and for confidence in God's justice.

Psalm 18:1-19

"Out of the deep waters"

Introduction: Psalm 18 is a royal psalm of thanksgiving, apparently for deliverance from a military defeat. Following a hymnic introduction (verses 2-4) is an account of what God did in mythic language (5-20). This is followed by the reasons why God came to the rescue (21-25). Then the story is repeated with a second introduction (26-35), which is followed by a more historical account of God's action (36-46). Finally, there is a closing proclamation of God's glory (47-50).

Preparation: When you are quiet and centered, recall a time in your life when you went through something very traumatic.

Read Psalm 18: (1-19) Read Psalm 18:1-19. Note the water imagery in verses 4-5 and 16.

Reflection: The overwhelming experiences of our lives are not usually accompanied with a trembling of the earth or thunder and lightning, at least not literally so. Yet, we have all had experiences which might be described poetically in such terms. The word *overwhelmed* means to be covered over or buried under as with water. Think of a time when you have been overwhelmed. Have you experienced a sense of being rescued by God from an "overwhelming" experience?

Prayer: Praise God for your own experience of being rescued from an overwhelming experience. Ask for the confidence to know that God will always be your protector.

Psalm 19:1-6

"Each day announces it to the following day"

Introduction:	Psalm 19 is a composite of two earlier psalms with different themes. Verses 1-6 were originally part of a call to praise God the Creator. The remainder of the psalm (verses 7-14) takes as its theme, "the law of the Lord." The first section speaks of God's glory as it is seen in the creation, specifically in the sky and the sun whose "voices" are heard in praise of God. There is a striking image in verse 2, "Each day announces it to the following day; each night repeats it to the next." The Hebrew word that is translated "announces" means something like "gurgles forth," as in a bubbling spring.
Preparation:	Relax in a comfortable place; release the tension in your body and let go of your inner tension. Imagine yourself in a favorite outdoor spot where you watch the sun rise, pass across the sky, and finally set in the west. After dark watch the moon come up.
Read Psalm 19: (1-6)	Read verses 1-6 at least twice.
Reflection:	What do the "voices" of the sun and moon sound like to you? How do you experience the glory of God in other ways in nature? How do you share it with others?
Prayer:	Give thanks to God for this reminder of the glory of God's creation. Ask God to help you carry this peace with you through the day.

Psalm 19:7-14

"Deliver me, Lord, from hidden faults"

Introduction:	While verses 1-6 and 7-14 began as different psalms, they are happily joined together. The first sings of God's glory in nature and the second of the glory of God's law, which provides us with strength, wisdom, happiness, and understanding. The law makes it possible for us to enjoy and preserve the wonder of creation.
Preparation:	Settle into the space you have chosen for your personal meditation. Take several deep breaths. Quiet any thoughts which intrude into this special time. With the Bible in your hand, remember some of its many and varied treasures: laws, sacred history, wisdom, proverbs, stories, prophetic calls to justice and righteousness, the good news of forgiveness, and advice to early churches.
Read Psalm 19: (7-14)	Read verses 7-14, pausing after each verse.
Reflection:	How are the laws of the Lord, "more desirable than the finest gold" and "sweeter than the purest honey"? How is one rewarded for obeying the laws of the Lord? Can you see the "hidden faults" of those you know well? What "hidden faults" might others see in you?
Prayer:	Make verses 12-14 the beginning of your own prayer. Add your own feelings and needs.

Psalm 20

"Some trust in their war chariots"

Introduction: This psalm was a prayer on behalf of a king prior to his going out to do battle. The first five verses ask for God's help and promise praise to God when the victory is won. The next three verses express confidence that God will grant victory to the king. Verse 7 may be an indication that the king expected to be outnumbered in battle. Taken as a whole the psalm reflects the "God is on our side" theology to which many resort in a time of national or international conflict. Yet, the first five verses may also be read as petitions on behalf of someone facing a personal crisis or a dangerous journey.

Preparation: Take plenty of time to quiet the tension within you. Recall a person who is facing overwhelming difficulties and prepare yourself to be in prayer on behalf of that person.

Read Psalm 20: Read the psalm slowly, giving attention first to verses 1-5; then verses 6-8; and finally, verse 9. Pause and then read it again, listening for thoughts or phrases which speak to you.

Reflection: Can you pray in confidence for someone in crisis? How do you feel about praying for God to be on your side in battle? What does verse 7 have to say to you? to Congress? to your political party? to the Pentagon?

Prayer: Pray for a person who is struggling with a problem. Pray also for the nations of the world that seem to be poised on the brink of battle.

Psalm 22

"Why have you abandoned me?"

Introduction: Christians associate Psalm 22 with Jesus dying on the cross. But it is the prayer for one who is gravely ill. The symptoms of the sickness are vividly given in verses 6-21. But, in words reminiscent of Job, the greatest suffering may be the matter of faith itself. In verses 22-31, perhaps later additions, the prayer is answered in a great thanksgiving banquet. Peace is found in the midst of suffering.

Preparation: Find the quiet center of prayer deep within your own spirit. Let go of the distracting thoughts and concerns of the day. Let your mind be open and empty.

Read Psalm 22: Read verses 1-21 more than once, until you feel some identity with the psalmist.

Reflection: Have you experienced others making light of your faith? Have you ever experienced such a feeling of abandonment by God and friends? Read verses 22-31. Recall a time when your faith was shaken by doubts and then suddenly returned because of changed circumstances.

Prayer: Express your feelings to God. What needs to happen to strengthen your faith? Celebrate the greatness of God, even when you can't feel it.

Psalm 23

"I have everything I need"

Introduction: For most Christians and Jews, this is the most beloved of all the psalms. It was used in early "Easter Vigil" services as new Christians proceeded from the water of baptism to their first Eucharist. It is built on the image of the shepherd and may have influenced Jesus' parable about his being the good shepherd. The shepherd image is strong in verses 1-3, after which it begins to dissolve. The metaphor is totally abandoned with verse 5 and is replaced by the image of a great banquet. Note also that God is spoken of in the third person until verse 5, when a shift is made to the greater intimacy of the second person.

Preparation: Clear your mind and schedule, allowing plenty of time for this favorite psalm. Relax and open yourself to the intimate presence of God deep within your own spirit.

Read Psalm 23: Read the entire psalm reflectively. Then wait for a moment or two before returning to it. Now take time to linger over each of the six verses.

Reflection: How do you feel about the phrase, "I have everything I need"? (compare with Psalm 16:5) Do you feel God's protection even in the "deepest darkness"? How does the psalm inspire complete confidence for you?

Prayer: Pray the psalm by reading each verse and responding to it.

Psalm 24

"Who has the right . . . ?"

Introduction: Possibly written to celebrate a military victory, this psalm was later adapted as a hymn in celebration of God's creation of the universe. Verses 1-2 are a hymn; verses 3-6 may reflect a ceremony of admittance to the Temple; and verses 7-10 continue the procession with attention directed to the Lord. Taken as a whole, Psalm 24 is one of the greatest literary compositions of the psalter.

Preparation: Quietly settle into your private time and space for prayer. Imagine yourself at a great religious festival. A huge crowd is present. Suddenly, there is a flourish of trumpets, and everyone bursts into song, singing this great hymn of creation.

Read Psalm 24: Read the psalm as if you were part of a large gathering of worshipers singing with great joy in a procession to the Temple.

Reflection: How do you "image" some of the events of creation? Who *does* have the right to "enter God's holy Temple"? How do you feel as one who has this privilege? How do you imagine the scene as the procession enters the Temple?

Prayer: Give thanks for the sense of awe and wonder in worship. Ask God to guide you, that you may always be worthy to "go up the Lord's hill."

Psalm 25

"Do not remember the sins of my youth" (NRSV)

Introduction: Psalm 25 is an acrostic poem, which means that each succeeding verse begins with the next letter of the Hebrew alphabet. Nevertheless, it maintains a remarkable thematic unity even in translation. Originally an individual lament, it was adapted for communal use, including the addition of the final verse. The author was conscious of personal sin, calling upon God for forgiveness and instruction.

Preparation: Experiment with different times of day for your praying of the psalms. You may also find that different kinds of psalms lend themselves to being read or prayed in different places.

Read Psalm 25: Read the psalm slowly; then after a brief silence, go back and read it again, pausing to reflect between stanzas.

Reflection: What phrases struck you as you read the psalm? Why? Why is an adult concerned about the "sins of my youth"? The psalmist refers several times to God's *teaching.* How do you think God teaches you? Can you identify with the psalmist's asking for relief from worry, loneliness, weakness, danger, and suffering?

Prayer: Ask God to forgive the sins of *your* youth and to teach *you* the right way.

Psalm 26

"O Lord, I love the house in which you dwell" (NRSV)

Introduction: At first impression this psalm seems to reflect a piety of great self-righteousness. But there are also indications of a deep humility in verses 2, 9, and 11. Perhaps the psalmist is consciously aware of self-righteous tendencies and is praying for mercy. On the other hand, there is another possible explanation for the tone of this psalm. Verses 6-8 may indicate that it was used regularly by a priest as part of the ritual cleansing before entering the Temple.

Preparation: After you center yourself for praying this psalm, ask yourself what attitude you bring to the prayer. Ask God to take away any self-righteousness in you and to help you approach your prayer in a humble spirit.

Read Psalm 26: Read the psalm slowly to get a feel for its content and flow. Then read it a second time to understand the feelings of the psalmist.

Reflection: With which lines of the psalm do you identify most strongly? How do you react to the spirituality of the psalmist? What does your reaction have to say about your own spirituality? How do you think other people perceive your spirituality?

Prayer: Ask God to help you better understand the attitudes you bring to your prayer.

Psalm 27:1-6

"I have asked the Lord for one thing"

Introduction:	Psalm 27 was originally two psalms (verses 1-6 and 7-14), later joined together with a common theme. In the first part of the psalm, the author looks to literal or figurative protection in the Temple.
Preparation:	Recalling a time when you felt surrounded by too many responsibilities or too much stress, imagine yourself on a high rock in the mountains, above the cares and strains of daily life. The air is fresh; the only sound is that of a gentle breeze blowing through the trees. Take time to enjoy this setting as you let go of your worries.
Read Psalm 27: (1-6)	Read the first six verses of the psalm as you sit in the security of your mountain.
Reflection:	In times of great stress, what is the "one thing" you would ask of the Lord? What would it be like to live in a truly secure place? Would regular visits to the security of your mountain help to reduce the stress in your life?
Prayer:	Ask God for the one thing you really need. How could you learn to live in "the Lord's house" all of your life? Thank God for this experience of peace and security.

Psalm 27:7-14

"Don't leave me, don't abandon me"

Introduction: The second part of Psalm 27 very likely originated as a separate psalm of lament. The word *abandon* is used three times and seems to represent the feeling of the psalmist. The psalmist anxiously prays that God's presence will not be withheld.

Preparation: Recall a time when you felt all alone, perhaps feeling abandoned by friends or co-workers. Get in touch with the yearning for someone to be with you.

Read Psalm 27: (7-14) Read the psalm slowly; pay attention to phrases and images that strike you, and linger over them. Read the psalm a second time.

Reflection: What phrase or idea presented itself to you most strongly? Why? Have you ever felt abandoned either physically or emotionally? Have you ever felt abandoned because you took an unpopular position about something? What would you like God to teach you to do in such a situation?

Prayer: Share with God a feeling you have had of being abandoned, especially if you have felt abandoned by God. Ask for the faith and strength to remain strong and whole even in the midst of such feelings.

Psalm 28

"They take no notice"

Introduction: The author of this lament does not give a specific reason for the prayer. Nevertheless, the Lord is addressed and asked for help. The request not to be condemned with the wicked, who "take no notice" of what the Lord has done, assumes that the wicked will be punished in the shadow world of the dead. Having received assurance from the priest, the psalmist offers praise to God (verses 6-8) and closes with a prayer for others as well (verse 9).

Preparation: Ask yourself why you want to pray. When you have answered that question, still your mind and body, asking for the privilege of being in God's presence.

Read Psalm 28: As always, read the psalm two times, slowly and reflectively.

Reflection: Have you ever felt that God was not answering your prayer? What did it feel like? Have you felt that your prayer was answered when you least expected it? How would you describe the differences between yourself and "the wicked"? Have you ever taken "no notice of what the Lord has done"?

Prayer: Ask God's forgiveness for your spiritual laziness which has resulted in your "taking no notice" of what God has done. Give praise for the blessings you have taken for granted.

Psalm 29

"The God of glory thunders" (NRSV)

Introduction: Psalm 29 is based on an unusual weather pattern related to the geography of the Middle East. Thunderstorms often come eastward across the Mediterranean Sea and strike the coast of Israel near the northern border with Lebanon; the storms continue east until they are deflected southward by Mount Hermon; then they encounter the dry air of the Arabian desert which keeps the storms turning until they pass *west* over the Negeb desert, south of Jerusalem and return back to the sea! This psalm is an account of the storm's progress as it passes all the way around Jerusalem!

Preparation: Gently center yourself. Remember a time when you sat quietly and observed a storm pass by in the distance.

Read Psalm 29: Read the psalm, paying attention to the geographical features mentioned as well as to the allusions to the "voice of the Lord."

Reflection: Imagine yourself on a hilltop in Jerusalem watching the storm thunder in from the sea west of you, pass by you to the north, behind you to the east, and finally, turn west again until it moves back out to sea. Listen to the "voice of the Lord" in the thunder. Feel the peace that comes when the storm has passed all around you and all is quiet.

Prayer: Give thanks for the glory of God as it is seen in nature and for the reminder that nature calls us to experience God's peace.

Psalm 30

"Tears in the night, joy in the morning"

Introduction:	The psalmist, possibly a priest in the Temple, has just survived a brush with death, perhaps by sudden recovery from an illness thought to be fatal, and is now overflowing with praise and thanksgiving for being spared.
Preparation:	Recall a time when you or someone you know came close to death by illness or accident and was spared. Center yourself quietly, concentrating on the life-giving breath that enters your lungs with so little effort on your part.
Read Psalm 30:	Read the psalm slowly. Feel the emotion of the psalmist sharing this experience. Read it a second time.
Reflection:	Have you ever experienced a brush with death? Do you remember a moment of sudden panic or hours of lingering fear? What does it feel like to be spared when you thought there was no hope? How do you feel about the second part of verse 5: "Tears may flow in the night, but joy comes in the morning"? Think about how fragile life really is. Did you have a need to tell others about it?
Prayer:	Give thanks to God for protecting you, even when you are not aware of it. Give thanks for all the life that has come to and through you since that time when you feared you would die. Praise God for life!

Psalm 31

"I am like something thrown away"

Introduction: A number of things about this psalm have led some scholars to believe that it is a composite of several other psalms, with some parts coming from the Book of Jeremiah as well. Some have even suggested that it would be divided into two psalms (verses 1-8 and verses 9-24). The beginning of verse 5 was quoted by Jesus on the cross and is often used by Christians as part of their evening prayer. Verses 9-20 describe the cruel persecution the psalmist has experienced in the past and perhaps is experiencing again in the present. Some of the details of this description leads us to believe that the psalmist may have been a leper.

Preparation: This psalm is the prayer of one whose personal situation has necessitated a complete reliance on God. Try to open yourself to this experience as you get ready to pray the psalm.

Read Psalm 31: You may need to read this psalm several times to become familiar with its content and to feel comfortable with its ragged flow of ideas.

Reflection: Can you identify with the experience of the psalmist, who has been so cruelly treated by others, yet who can find protection and security in God? How do you feel about the contrast between "I am like something thrown away" in verse 12*b* and "I am always in your care" in verse 15*a?*

Prayer: Commend yourself to God's care, *whatever* you face in your life.

Psalm 32

"Don't be stupid like a horse or a mule"

Introduction: This is probably a psalm which was used for the corporate worship of God in the Temple in Jerusalem. It reflects a service of thanksgiving after a public confession of sin and the proclamation of God's forgiveness.

> verses 1-2: a canticle of blessedness spoken by a priest;
> verses 3-5: the confession of sin;
> verses 6-7: a prayer of assurance and confidence in God's love;
> verses 8-10: a short sermon;
> verse 11: a congregational response of praise.

Preparation: When you are centered give yourself permission to enjoy the silence a few moments without feeling the need to *do* something.

Read Psalm 32: Pause to reflect on the verses and ideas that strike you.

Reflection: What are the problems or "sins" that burden your life because you have refused to own them, confess them, and accept responsibility for them? What things do you especially need to confess to God? Do it. In what ways are you stupid or stubborn "like a horse or mule"? What is it like to experience forgiveness? to offer it to others?

Prayer: Offer to God your feelings; admit those things that get in the way in your life; ask for God's forgiveness.

Psalm 33

"War horses are useless for victory"

Introduction: This is a wisdom psalm and reminds us of the need to put things in perspective. The *Lord* is the creator and protector of the earth. Kings, soldiers, and armies do not win because of their might, but because they are just and righteous.

Preparation: Time and space are important for meditation. Choose a time when you are alert and open to hear God's word for you. (After lunch is usually *not* a good time, because we become drowsy.) Choose a place where you feel relaxed and comfortable, away from distractions such as the telephone.

Read Psalm 33: Read the psalm slowly and prayerfully. Give yourself a moment or two of silence and then read it again. Open yourself to hear the distilled wisdom of our spiritual ancestors.

Reflection: Why do the righteous give praise to the Lord? How do the psalmist's feelings about armies and war horses relate to our modern military establishment? Does our nation place its hope more in military solutions than it does on righteousness and justice?

Prayer: Give thanks to God for God's constant love, righteousness, and justice. Add your own feelings and insights from your meditation.

Psalm 34

"Come, my young friends"

Introduction: This is another example of a wisdom psalm. It appears to be the work of an older person reflecting on a life of faith. The psalmist wants to share what has been learned with those who are younger. The theme of God's care is prominent. *"[God's] angel guards those who honor the Lord"*; *"The Lord watches over the righteous and listens to their cries"*; *"[God] rescues them from all their troubles"*; *"The Lord is near to those who are discouraged."*

Preparation: A secret of prayer is learning how to clear the mind of its habit of jumping from one thought to another. We speak of this jumping about as our "mind wandering." Try to focus your mind on *one* simple thing; count your breaths up to four, over and over. Your mind will still wander to other thoughts, but gently let them go and return to counting your breaths. This discipline takes time, but it eventually teaches us to clear our minds for prayer.

Read Psalm 34: As you read the psalm, note the questions in verse 12.

Reflection: Have you ever had the feeling that God was watching over you? How does this relate to the psalmist's speaking of having a guardian angel?

Prayer: Be thankful for God's constant care for you . . . even when you are not aware of it. And your own thoughts and prayers.

Psalm 35

"Without any reason they laid a trap for me"

Introduction: Psalm 35 is a personal lament of one who has been unjustly accused by former friends. Parts of the psalm seem vindictive to our modern ears, even to the point of calling for the offenders to be disgraced. The psalmist is asking for justice to be done in a public way because of the public nature of the injustice that was done. Note that the author's praise of God seems to be conditional upon God's taking action against those who perpetrated the injustice.

Preparation: Most of us find it easy to avoid praying when we "don't feel like it." Thus we need to guard against our spiritual laziness and discipline ourselves to take time for prayer regularly. Being faithful to the process opens us to the riches of God's grace.

Read Psalm 35: Read the psalm more than once, listening carefully to the feelings of the author. Watch for feelings which are similar to feelings you have or have had.

Reflection: Are you tempted in your prayers to tell God what to do? Do you think the attitudes of the psalmist contribute to a possible reconciliation with those who have been unjust or make that reconciliation more unlikely? What do you think the psalmist should have been praying for?

Prayer: Recalling a time when you were angry at another person or persons, pray for the maturity to see your own faults as well as those of others.

Psalm 36

"Your constant love reaches the heavens"

Introduction: This is a beautiful psalm contrasting the goodness of God with our human shortcomings. The psalmist is aware of how evil works in us to deceive us. The second part of the psalm (verses 5-12) speaks of the love, faithfulness, righteousness, and justice of God. Verse 7 contains the Hebrew word *hesed*, usually translated *constant* or *steadfast*, referring to the quality of God's love. The word also means merciful and faithful. It is found often in the Psalms.

Preparation: Quiet your body and your spirit. Allow the silence to penetrate into your heart and bring you a sense of peace.

Read Psalm 36: Read verses 1-4; reflect on them a moment or two. Then, read the entire psalm.

Reflection: How does the psalmist's description of our humanness fit with your own experience? How do you feel about the contrast between human nature and the goodness of God? What can you do to bring your own life into closer harmony with God's will?

Prayer: Share your feelings with God in an informal way. Confess your shortcomings; ask God for forgiveness and for the grace to bring your actions into harmony with your ideals.

Psalm 37

"Righteousness . . . like the noonday sun"

Introduction: This psalmist tries to answer the timeless questions, "Why do the good suffer and the wicked prosper"? The psalm, another alphabetical acrostic, is really a collection of proverbs or wise sayings, though the theme remains consistent throughout. It is the advice of an old man (verse 25) to those who are younger and less experienced. The argument is that *in the long run* the righteous will prosper and the wicked will be punished.

Preparation: One of the primary messages of this psalm is patience . . . perhaps even life-long patience. Therefore, we are well advised to pray it patiently. Give yourself plenty of time to find the quiet place deep within yourself.

Read Psalm 37: Read the psalm through the first time to become familiar with the general outline of its argument. Then allow yourself some quiet time before reading it a second time.

Reflection: Do you wonder sometimes if righteousness really pays off? Do you ever feel jealous of those who gain in position and material things by less than honorable means? Do you ever compromise your own standards because "everybody else is doing it"? How does your life witness to others?

Prayer: Let your prayer flow out of the feelings which the psalm has generated in you.

Psalm 38

"Because I have been foolish"

Introduction:	Here we have the prayer of one who is very sick. The person assumes that the disease is a result of "foolish" deeds and perhaps has been caused by God as a punishment for sin. Even so, the one who is sick has confidence that God will answer.
Preparation:	Open your mind and heart to the presence of God's gentle spirit. Sit quietly until you are free of distractions.
Read Psalm 38:	Try to get inside the mind and body of the psalmist, sensing the pain and burden of suffering because of one's own sin.
Reflection:	Have you had experiences when you felt that you were being punished because of your own foolish actions? When suffering is the result of one's own actions, what is the role of God in it? What is it like to trust in God's love even when you feel God has caused your pain? What part does guilt play in such feelings? What is to be learned from such an experience?
Prayer:	Ask God for a deeper understanding of human suffering. Give thanks for the continuing love of God even when we are in the midst of great pain.

Psalm 39

"I will keep quiet, I will not say a word"

Introduction: Psalm 39 is a poignant prayer of someone who is apparently suffering a terminal illness. The psalmist exhibits anger against God. Indeed some would say that the prayer is an effort to manipulate or bargain with God. There is some sense of acceptance in the final verses. It is a psalm filled with the anguish that many experience under such circumstances.

Preparation: Preparing oneself to pray this psalm involves not only the matter of centering, but the willingness to struggle with some painful human feelings which most of us would rather avoid. Give yourself permission to look at your feelings about your own death.

Read Psalm 39: Read the psalm carefully to get a sense of its flow and content. Then go back and read it again, taking time to hear the subtle things going on in the mind of the psalmist.

Reflection: What specific emotions can you identify in this psalm? Who is responsible for the suffering the psalmist feels? Did the author's self-imposed silence serve a valid purpose? How do you feel about verse 12? Could you ease the burden of someone suffering in this way by engaging him or her in a meaningful dialogue about it?

Prayer: Ask God to help you understand the complex feelings we all have about our own certain death. Ask for the grace to be open about such feelings when the time comes.

Psalm 40

"Out of a dangerous pit"

Introduction: Psalm 40 is a combination of two earlier psalms. The first is found in verses 1-11. This is followed by another psalm (verses 12-17), which is duplicated in Psalm 70. The opening verses constitute an exceptionally fine prayer: God saves us, rescues us, and teaches us a "new song." Today's English Version and some other translations speak of God pulling us out of the *pit*—not literally a hole in the ground, but rather "the pits" or some "pitfall" we have gotten ourselves into. God does not ask for animal sacrifices, but simply for us to keep God's teachings.

Preparation: Center yourself, clearing your mind of tensions and extraneous concerns. Relax your body. Know that you are doing something important.

Read Psalm 40: Read verses 1-11 at least twice.

Reflection: What is it in your life that is "the pits"? What are your pitfalls? How did you get there? Do you remember a time when you were "rescued from the pit"?

Prayer: Share with God what in your life is the pits. Ask God's help in getting out. Listen to hear what you need to do to help yourself. Give thanks for God's constant love.

Psalm 41

"Restore my health"

Introduction: Those who are or have been seriously ill will relate well to this psalm. It is the prayer of a sick person. As such it contains a whole range of feelings and moods. There is evidence of true humility and righteousness in the prayer. But, there are also lines in which the psalmist, like many of us, seems to wallow in the illness, crying "poor me." Like many who are sick, the psalmist feels shunned or ignored by good friends and turns to God as the one who will always be faithful.

Preparation: Reflect on your growing experience of praying the psalms. What do you need to do to enhance the quality of your prayer? Is the time and place adequate? Do you need to change something (posture, attitude, surroundings) to make it a better experience?

Read Psalm 41: Let it be *your own* prayer.

Reflection: What feelings expressed in the prayer did you identify with? Does our feeling sorry for ourselves sometimes cause our friends to turn away from us? If you are (or were) ill, how would your own prayer differ from this one?

Prayer: Offer to God the fruits of your reading and reflection of this psalm: what you have learned, what you have felt. Give thanks for God's constant love and care for you.

Psalms 42/43

"As a deer longs for . . . cool water"

Introduction: Psalms 42 and 43 were originally a single unified lament, later divided by an ancient editor for reasons unknown. Note the repetition of phrases and questions in the two psalms. Taken as a whole it is the prayer of one in exile someplace to the north, perhaps in the northern part of the Jordan valley, near Mount Hermon. The psalmist recalls vividly past experiences of going to pray in the Temple in Jerusalem and longs, like "a deer longs for a stream of cool water," to worship the Lord again in Jerusalem.

Preparation: "Take time to be holy." Remind yourself that you deserve this special time apart from all the rush and routine of daily life.

Read Psalms
42/43: Linger over those phrases which speak of loneliness and exile.

Reflection: Remember a time when you were a long way from home and felt lonely. Experience the *feeling* of "longing" for a favorite place where you have experienced interior peace. What would it be like to go back to that place again? What keeps you from going there?

Prayer: Thank God for special places and times of security and peace. Ask God to help you to experience such peace where you are right now.

Psalm 44

"You have made us a joke among the nations"

Introduction: Psalm 44 is the lament of a nation after defeat in battle. The people complain bitterly that God did not protect Israel. The nation, recalling its own faithfulness, feels unjustly abandoned by God and calls for God to "wake up" and come to Israel's aid. The people wonder what it means to be God's chosen people.

Preparation: Most of us give at least minimal attention to our physical and emotional health. Yet, we often neglect our spiritual health which is nurtured in silence, prayer, and listening.

Read Psalm 44: Read the psalm slowly to get a sense of its content. Then go back and read it again, listening for the feelings and thoughts expressed by the people.

Reflection: If you experienced or have heard about the turmoil of the American people during and following the Vietnam War, you may have a better understanding of this psalm. The Vietnam experience caused Americans to question many of their previous assumptions, resulting in emotions including anger, denial, and guilt. The nation felt abandoned by God and did not examine its own failures. How can we avoid making an idol of the nation?

Prayer: Share with God your feelings about the relationship of nations (especially your own) to God. Ask for greater understanding and clarity.

Psalm 46

"Even if the earth is shaken"

Introduction: Psalm 46 speaks of Jerusalem as the refuge where God's people are safe "even if the earth is shaken." Whatever happens in the upheavals of the world, Jerusalem will be safe. It is the psalm that inspired Martin Luther's hymn, "A Mighty Fortress Is Our God." The psalm may date from the time of King Hezekiah under whose rule Jerusalem escaped destruction by the Assyrians. If so, the "river that brings joy to the city of God" could be a reference to the Gihon Spring which, located outside the city wall, was Jerusalem's only source of water. The water was brought into the city to the Pool of Siloam through "Hezekiah's Tunnel."

Preparation: As you center yourself for praying this psalm, think of a place where you have felt absolutely safe and secure.

Read Psalm 46: Feel the strength of this psalm as you read it.

Reflection: Can you affirm with the psalmist that "we will not be afraid, even if the earth is shaken and the mountains fall into the ocean depths"? Is there in your own spirituality, "a river that brings joy to the city of God"?

Prayer: As you pray, be honest with God about your fears, about the earthshaking events in your life. Can you pray: "God is our shelter and strength, always ready to help in times of trouble"?

Psalm 48

"Walk around Zion and count the towers"

Introduction: Those who have visited and are familiar with the old city of Jerusalem will recognize the feelings evoked by this psalm. The psalm recalls God's defeat of those who came to attack Jerusalem, built on Mount Zion, "the mountain of God." The city with its high walls and towers is a symbol of God's strength and greatness. God's people are urged to walk about the walls and count the towers which provide security such that "this God is our God forever and ever." Secure inside the Temple, the people meditate on God's constant love.

Preparation: In the nuclear age no city is safe from destruction. Thus, we have to imagine such a secure city, high on a mountain, with invincible walls.

Read Psalm 48: Read the psalm noting:
verses 1-3:   in praise of God's holy mountain;
verses 4-8:   the defeat of enemy kings;
verses 9-11: God's love and justice;
verses 12-14: the security of the fortress.

Reflection: In spite of its walls, Jerusalem was conquered and devastated many times. Is there wisdom in basing our security on the strength of our defenses, or does real security come from justice?

Prayer: Enter into a dialogue with God about what it is that constitutes *your* security.

Psalm 49

"The payment for a human life is too great"

Introduction:	Often called a wisdom psalm, this prayer invites us to reflect on the matter of our wealth and possessions. Verse 17 could well be the origin of our modern saying, "you can't take it with you."

verses 1-4:	Addressed to both the rich and the poor;
verses 7-9:	Life is more than one's possessions;
verses 10-12:	Riches cannot overcome death;
verses 17-20:	No one can carry wealth beyond death.

Preparation:	Have you thought about the term, *holy space*? For many of us the sanctuary of a church provides holy space. Do you have adequate holy space for your prayer? If not, what could you do to make it so?
Read Psalm 49:	Read the psalm through to get a sense of its meaning. Reflect on it for two or three minutes. Then go back and read it again slowly, watching for phrases that speak to you today.
Reflection:	What are your real feelings about money? How often do you worry about it? How much do you depend on money for your security? How would you pay the price for your life?
Prayer:	Begin your prayer with your reflections on the questions above.

Psalm 50

"Let the giving of thanks be your sacrifice"

Introduction: Here is a psalm which has a prophetic ring to it. It recalls a ceremony in which the Lord inquires about the faithfulness of the people. Though it takes place on Mount Zion, it is modeled after the experience of the Israelites at Mount Sinai. Verses 1-6 are a manifestation of God. In verses 7-15 God speaks to the people through a priest, saying in effect, make sure your sacrifices are motivated by *thankfulness* and not mere ritual. Verses 16-21 constitute a divine judgment upon those who have violated God's commands. The severe tone continues in the closing verses, but with the hope that those who repent will be saved.

Preparation: Prepare yourself for meditation in your accustomed way, but know that in this psalm you will be confronted with the question of the motivation behind your prayer.

Read Psalm 50: Read each section prayerfully, pausing before going on to the next: verses 1-6, verses 7-15, verses 16-21, verses 22-23.

Reflection: How do you feel about your own patterns of worship? Are you motivated by habit, ritual, humility, thankfulness?

Prayer: Let your prayer be like an informal conversation with God. What questions does God address to you? How do you answer them?

Psalm 51

"I recognize my faults"

Introduction:	This is perhaps the most well-known of the penitential psalms. It begins by asking for mercy through the constant love of God (verses 1-2). Verses 3-6 are a confession of personal sin with the understanding that such sin has been an affront to God. The prayer for forgiveness continues in verses 7-9, followed by a desire for moral renewal (verses 10-12). Then follows the desire to share God's forgiveness with others. Verses 16-17 contain an idea, revolutionary at the time, that what God requires is not the traditional sacrifice of an animal, but a humble spirit. A later editor of the psalms tried to make it more acceptable by the addition of verses 18-19.
Preparation:	Sit in a quiet place for a few minutes; read the psalm slowly and reflectively, allowing it to speak to your own condition.
Read Psalm 51:	Read this psalm as if you had written it yourself.
Reflection:	Are you conscious of your own sins? Do you recognize your own faults? What would it be like to have such things removed that you might be "washed clean?" What is the "humble spirit" or "pure heart" that God requires of you?
Prayer:	Let your prayer flow out of your reflections and feelings.

Psalm 52

"Like an olive tree growing in the house of God"

Introduction: This psalm does not fit easily into most psalm types. It seems to be addressed to a person who derives great power and influence from wealth. It thus has the sense of a wisdom or teaching psalm that calls down the judgment of God on those who arrogantly rely on their own wealth, rather than on God. The attitude of the psalmist may seem self-righteous to modern ears, yet to the psalmist there was always the possibility that those who were "wicked" would become righteous, or for that matter, that the righteous might be tempted to the same arrogance in other circumstances.

Preparation: As we approach this and other psalms that seem to draw such sharp distinctions between the righteous and the wicked, it is important to remember not only that "there but for the grace of God go I," but also that God may well grace the "wicked one" with repentance and humility.

Read Psalm 52: Read the psalm first from the point of view of the person who wrote it; then read it a second time imagining yourself to be the wealthy person addressed.

Reflection: What is your attitude toward the arrogance of the rich and powerful? What does the image of the "olive tree growing in the house of God" mean to you?

Prayer: Pray for greater understanding of those who have wealth.

Psalm 54

"May God use their own evil to punish my enemies"

Introduction: Psalm 54 is typical of the psalms of personal lament. It is the prayer of one pursued by enemies. The Hebrew title associates it with Saul's pursuit of David, but we have no way of knowing if the psalm was actually written by David. The structure is simple:

verses 1-2:   Appeal to God for help;
verse 3:   Reason for the prayer;
verses 4-5:   Petition for help from God;
verses 6-7:   Thanksgiving for deliverance.

Preparation: As you prepare for this prayer, reflect on the overwhelming grace of spending time in God's presence.

Read Psalm 54: Read the psalm to sense its content and flow. Read it again as if you were the one who had written it.

Reflection: Have you ever felt pursued by someone who could harm you either physically or otherwise? Have you ever thought of other persons as evil, when the evil was at least as much your own fault as theirs? Can you remember being afraid of meeting someone you had offended but didn't get around to seeking reconciliation with? Have you ever made a promise to someone, but then let that person down, and then dreaded meeting him or her? Was that person pursuing you . . . or were you avoiding him or her?

Prayer: Ask God to take away your feeling of being pursued by giving you the courage to seek reconciliation with someone with whom you may be out of sorts for whatever reason.

Psalm 55

"His words were smoother than cream"

Introduction: The author of this psalm was one who faced anxiety, persecution, misfortune, and taunts from every side. The temptation to "fly away and find rest" is reminiscent of Psalm 11. Even the desert seemed more attractive than familiar surroundings, because the taunts come not from long-time enemies, but from a close friend and companion who betrayed the psalmist. The poignancy of the situation is well stated in verses 12-14.

Preparation: If you have ever been betrayed by a close friend, you will have little difficulty identifying with the author of this psalm.

Read Psalm 55: Read the psalm to become familiar with the *feelings* of the psalmist. Then read it a second time as a prayer.

Reflection: Have you ever experienced the bitterness of betrayal by a close friend? How do you feel about the harshness of verse 15? What do you think about the apparent resolution of the psalmist's feelings in verses 22-23?

Prayer: If you have ever experienced this situation, let it be the basis of your prayer. Ask God to keep you from betraying your friends.

Psalm 57

"In the shadow of your wings"

Introduction: According to tradition this psalm was written by David when he was hiding from Saul (1 Samuel 24). In any case, it is the story of one who finds refuge in God in the midst of great peril. "In the shadow of your wings" may be a simple metaphor for God's protection or it may refer to the wings of the cherubim which spread over the ark of the covenant in the inner chamber of the Temple.

Preparation: As you center yourself for praying this psalm, imagine yourself in a place where you feel especially secure.

Read Psalm 57: Read the psalm through for the first time. After a few moments read it again, paying special attention to the interwoven themes of confidence in God's protection and fear of enemies.

Reflection: As a result of personal conflicts, jealousies, and competition, most of us sometimes feel like we are "surrounded by enemies." Sometimes the situation seems all that much worse because of a paranoid response on our part. Can you recall a time when you felt that way? Do you remember times in your life when your mood has swung back and forth between confidence in God and fear of the circumstances swirling around you? What do you think the psalmist meant by "they dug a pit in my path, but fell into it themselves"?

Prayer: Pray this psalm today against the background of the stresses and conflicts of your life.

Psalm 58

"They tell lies from the day they are born"

Introduction: Psalm 58 is a lament against the tyranny of evildoers in the world. The author rails against corrupt judges. There is no forgiveness. Instead the psalmist offers classic cursings such as, "May they be like snails that dissolve into slime"! The final verses affirm the belief that God will "blow them away while they are still living" and that "the righteous will be glad" as they are rewarded with the knowledge that "there is indeed a God who judges the world."

Preparation: Take time to prepare yourself adequately for prayer. At the same time remember that prayer is not always easy, nor does it always focus on pleasant topics!

Read Psalm 58: Read the psalm through to become familiar with its content. Then, after a moment or two, go back and read it again to get in touch with its emotional impact.

Reflection: At first glance this psalm may appear to be without redeeming qualities. Yet, it reflects feelings which many of us experience. We have suffered the repeated lies of trusted presidents; we have seen more than enough of political corruption; we are surrounded by dishonest business and financial institutions; false advertising is almost taken for granted. Have we become so accustomed to such things that we are no longer capable of righteous anger? Are *you* immune from such corruption? Can you identify with the psalmist?

Prayer: Allow your prayer to struggle with these issues.

Psalm 59

"Their tongues are like swords in their mouths"

Introduction: Another individual lament, Psalm 59 is a companion to Psalm 58. In Psalm 58 the focus is on human corruption. In Psalm 59 the focus is on unsavory persons who seem not to care or perhaps even to be aware of the moral and social implications of their speech and actions. "Their tongues are like swords in their mouths, yet they think that no one hears them." The author is not only disgusted with such behavior but has been under personal attack by the same enemies.

Preparation: While such psalms may cause us to identify with the righteousness of the psalmist, we need to enter our prayer with humility before God. To pray is to open oneself to the possibility of confrontation with one's own sin.

Read Psalm 59: Read the psalm first to gain an overview of its content. Then read it one or two more times to get in touch with the feelings and theology of the author.

Reflection: Have you encountered people whose crude speech betrays a lack of sensitivity toward others? Do you ignore them? get angry at them? let them get under your skin? Might others have heard intemperate words from your mouth? Have you said things in anger or frustration which were harmful or disgusting to others?

Prayer: Ask God to help you to know how to respond and even help those whose "tongues are like swords in their mouths."

Psalm 60

"You have warned those who have reverence for you"

Introduction: Psalm 60 is a community lament over a national calamity, probably a military defeat with loss of territory. The defeat and its effects on the people are compared to an earthquake (verse 2). The prayer raises both military and religious questions. If the territories mentioned in verses 7-8 were lost in battle, the psalmist reminds the people that they are part of God's gift to the people of Israel and will be restored. The psalm ends with such an assurance.

Preparation: Just as we need to clear our minds of *personal* clutter before we pray, we also need to dismiss political clutter. A prayer for the nation also calls for humility and openness.

Read Psalm 60: Having read the introductory material, read the psalm first to understand what is being said and then a second time to identify some of the subtle theological assumptions.

Reflection: How do you feel about some of the psalmist's theological interpretations concerning God's role in Israel's defeat:

- "You have rejected us, God, and defeated us"
- "You have been angry with us . . . . "
- "You have made your people suffer greatly"
- "You have warned those who have reverence for you, so that they might escape destruction."

Are there comparisons you can draw between the national feelings of Israel in this psalm and the feelings of some persons in the United States after the withdrawal of U.S. troops from Vietnam?

Prayer: Let your prayer be a time of listening to God about such questions. What do you hear God saying?

Psalm 61

"In despair and far from home I call to you"

Introduction:	We cannot be certain what circumstances caused the author of this psalm to be "in despair and far from home." It may be the result of political exile or perhaps an illness which prevented the worshiper from praying in the Temple. In any case there is a sincere longing to be in the security of the Temple under the protection of the wings of the cherubim. The prayer for the king (verses 6-7) may well be a later addition and serves as a reminder to all of us to pray for those who are stewards of our national life.
Preparation:	Examine briefly your feelings about praying scripture as you prepare yourself. Do you approach it out of duty? joy? humility? expectation? boredom? faithfulness?
Read Psalm 61:	Try reading this psalm omitting verses 6-7. Can you identify with the feelings of the psalmist?
Reflection:	If you have a regular time and an accustomed place for prayer, you have likely experienced a sense of disruption when you have been away from home for a time. Remember such a time and your longing for your usual place of prayer. To what extent is your experience of God tied to a familiar place? Is your sense of God's protection related to a particular place?
Prayer:	Let your reflections be the springboard for your prayer. Ask God to help you expand the geographical bounds of your prayer life.

Psalm 62

"Like a puff of breath"

Introduction: Most of us have had the experience of being attacked or abandoned by those we thought were friends. This psalm seems to be directed to those who have made life hard for the author. It is a mature reflection on the experience of being the victim of "two-faced" friends. One is not to trust in such persons, in violence, or in money, but only in the constant love of God. It is the reflection of one who has been through a lot, has survived with a strong faith, and now holds the conviction that God will continue to be there, no matter what.

Preparation: Remember some of the trials and tribulations of your own life. Friends do not always come through for us. Little in human terms can be taken for granted. Quietly center yourself and be open to the presence of the God who is completely dependable.

Read Psalm 62: Read the psalm through twice, trying to feel what its author felt. Pause to savor phrases which speak to you now.

Reflection: Do you ever speak to someone with "words of blessing" while privately cursing that person in your heart? What do you think about the statement that people "are all like a puff of breath"? Are we not a puff of God's breath (*ruach*), breathed into us at creation?

Prayer: Give thanks for God's steadfastness of love which holds us even when other people don't really care.

Psalm 63

"My soul is thirsty for you"

Introduction:	Psalm 63 is an intensely personal prayer. It is almost like a love poem, reminiscent in some ways of the Song of Songs (or Song of Solomon). As such it seems to end with verse 8. The final verses may be later additions, perhaps showing the contrast of those who do not know the love of God.
Preparation:	Most of us have "mountaintop experiences" when God is intimately present to us. We also have dry periods when God seems to be far away. As you center yourself for prayer, be aware of who God is for *you* right now.
Read Psalm 63:	Read the psalm, giving special attention to the *feelings* expressed by the psalmist. Read it a second time, with attention to *your own* feelings.
Reflection:	Have you ever felt that your spiritual life was "like a dry, worn-out, and waterless land"? Are there particular times in your day when you long for God? Is there a sanctuary or other place where you feel especially close to God? Have you ever prayed before going to sleep and then awakened in the night and felt as if you were still praying?
Prayer:	Let your prayer focus on your search for God as you are at this time in your life.

Psalm 64

"They . . . aim cruel words like arrows"

Introduction: Here is another individual lament by someone who has suffered at the hands of those who engage in plots, cruel words, shameless lies, and slander (verses 2-6). The second part of the psalm affirms that those who "aim cruel words like arrows" will themselves be the victims of God's arrows. Good people will rejoice and offer praise for God's justice.

Preparation: The effects of words can be harmful or healing—even the words we choose for our prayers or the words in our minds as we come to the experience of prayer. It is best to clear away the words in our minds so that we can simply listen to the Word.

Read Psalm 64: This psalm is simple and straightforward. Still, it is best to read it more than once. In your second or third reading, notice all the action verbs.

Reflection: Most of us have not been the victim of a plot. But, we may well have experienced the pain of another's sharp tongue, "cruel words," "shameless lies," or "cowardly slander." Sometimes we react defensively. Sometimes we simply "consider the source." What about our own cruel words? Such words spoken in confidence often have a way of getting back to those we spoke about with devastating results. Are these results "God's arrows"?

Prayer: In your prayer, ask God for increased sensitivity to the power of words, especially your own words.

Psalm 65

"The whole world stands in awe"

Introduction: This great hymn of thanksgiving was part of the temple liturgy. Perhaps it was written to celebrate the return of rain after a drought. While it opens with references to the Temple in Jerusalem, it continues with a more universal outlook including "people all over the world." There is a wonderful contrast between the "roar of the seas" in verse 7 and showers which "soften the soil" in verse 10.

Preparation: As you clear your mind and spirit of the clutter of the day, try to place yourself in your favorite pastoral scene at harvest time.

Read Psalm 65: Read the psalm first to become aware of its rich imagery; then read it a second time as you would sing a great hymn of thanksgiving.

Reflection: What are some of the gifts of God named in the psalm? Take a few moments to imagine a gentle rain falling on the plowed fields. Can you hear the flocks and even the land itself shouting and singing for joy! How do you respond to "Our faults defeat us, but you forgive them"?

Prayer: Let your prayer flow out of your reflections as you give thanks to God.

Psalm 66

"I will give you what I said I would"

Introduction: This psalm from the temple liturgy is introduced by a choral hymn (verses 1-7). Then follows a corporate prayer of thanksgiving (verses 8-12), which recalls some of the nation's more difficult times that have finally ended with God bringing the people to a place of safety. The final words of thanksgiving are in the first person.

Preparation: How do you approach your time of praying with the scriptures? Has it become a stale habit? Perhaps you need to find a new *place* for your prayer or a new *time.*

Read Psalm 66: When you are centered, read Psalm 66, taking note of its three major parts. After a few moments, read it again, allowing significant phrases to suggest themselves to you.

Reflection: Recall some of the difficult times our Hebrew ancestors went through with their God. How had God tested the people? How has God tested you? What kind of offering do you bring to God? What have you said you would give to God, that you now need to give?

Prayer: Let your prayer be a personal response to some of these questions shared with God.

Psalm 67

"May all the peoples praise you"

Introduction: This song of thanksgiving used for congregational worship is a gem among the psalms for its brevity, structure, and universal spirit. It opens with the well-known priestly blessing found in Numbers 6:24-25. The blessing is affirmed by the people in verse 2. Then follows the first refrain (verse 3), followed by the affirmation that the Lord guides all nations. The second refrain is found in verse 5, after which the blessing of the harvest is acknowledged.

Preparation: As you prepare to pray this psalm, try to rise above the mindset of geographical boundaries that often limits the scope of our thoughts, and think of the world blessed by God, who is just to all peoples.

Read Psalm 67: Read the psalm, imagining yourself part of a large congregation hearing the opening verse chanted by the leader and the refrains sung by the entire congregation.

Reflection: Think about how the generous spirit of this psalm might be made a part of your life this day. In an age of technological wonders it is so easy to forget that everything we have comes from God, rather than a factory.

Prayer: Read the psalm again, making it your own prayer; then add your own personal thanksgiving.

Psalm 68:4-10, 32-35

"O God, when you led your people"

Introduction: Scholars have long debated over the text of Psalm 68. It is likely that it is composed of fragments of a number of earlier psalms. It revolves around the theme of a great march, beginning with a quotation of Moses when the ark of the covenant was moved (Numbers 10:35). Verses 7-10 recall Israel's life in the desert. Verses 11-14 have to do with the conquest of the promised land. Next comes the march to Jerusalem in verses 15-18. The psalm culminates with a temple procession. The psalm thus recounts the evolution of Israel's worship from the desert to urban worship (at the Temple).

Preparation: As you ready yourself to pray a part of Psalm 68, be aware that your prayer joins the prayers of your spiritual ancestors in the desert and in Jerusalem over untold generations.

Read Psalm 68: (4-10, 32-35) Because this psalm is long and complex, read only verses 4-10 and 32-35.

Reflection: "O God, when you led your people" is an invitation to recall our history, just like "Once upon a time" or "Long, long ago and far, far away." Take time to remember some of our ancient salvation history. Can you think of ways in which we recognize God leading us in the contemporary world?

Prayer: Let your prayer be one of praise and thanksgiving for God's being with us from the desert to the city.

Psalm 69

"There is no solid ground"

Introduction: Psalm 69 is a personal lament of unusual length that combines confession, prayer, anger, desperation, anguish of pain, and even thanksgiving for anticipated relief. The suffering of the psalmist is both metaphorical (verses 1-3) and real (verses 4-12). In the author's view the suffering is a result of devotion to God, which has brought insult after insult. The water metaphor that begins the psalm is continued in the prayer for help in verses 14-15. There is an extensive call for God to punish those responsible for the author's suffering (verses 22-28). The psalm closes with praise and thanksgiving for God's expected action.

Preparation: Having prepared yourself for the praying of this psalm, recall a time when you felt overwhelmed by the circumstances of your life and became deeply discouraged.

Read Psalm 69: While the psalm is lengthy, it is worth repeated reading.

Reflection: Read again the two opening verses and reflect on the phrases that we still hear from those in our own time who feel overwhelmed. What evidence is there that the author of this psalm accepted some responsibility for the situation? How does the psalmist feel about God? How would you feel about God in similar circumstances?

Prayer: If you have lived through a similar experience, recall it in God's presence and reflect on your reaction to it. Ask God to be with someone you know who is overwhelmed.

Psalm 71

"I am old and my hair is gray"

Introduction: This psalm is the prayer of an older person who, apparently persecuted by enemies, seeks refuge in the Temple. Contained within the prayer are allusions to Psalms 22, 31, 35, and 40. It is a passionate cry to God for help and, at the same time, an expression of feeling secure with God, learned from a lifetime of praising God. Such faith will overcome the power of those who seek to harm.

Preparation: Those who have lived long enough to have gray hair will have little trouble praying this psalm. Younger persons might want to remember the faith they have seen expressed so freely and simply by an elderly person they know.

Read Psalm 71: Read the psalm to get a feel for its overall meaning. Then go back and read it a second time, trying to identify with the perspective of the one with gray hair who wrote it.

Reflection: Have you noticed that many older persons seem to be able to express their faith more easily than those who are younger? How do you feel about maturity? Have you sometimes felt that you have achieved it, only to discover a few years later that you are still growing? Notice in verse 7 that the psalmist gives God credit for lifelong accomplishments.

Prayer: Share with God your own feelings about aging. Pray for those who are elderly and ask to learn from their example.

Psalm 72

"Like rain on the fields"

Introduction: Used for royal festivals at the Temple in Jerusalem, this psalm is a prayer asking that the king might be one through whom God's justice and righteousness is made available, not only to God's people, but to the very land itself. "May the king be like rain on the fields" sets a high standard for any ruler, ancient or modern!

Preparation: When you have temporarily dismissed the concerns of the day and centered yourself in the presence of God, imagine yourself present at the inauguration of a president. You are the one who will give the benediction and this psalm is your prayer.

Read Psalm 72: Read the psalm as if you were praying it for a president just beginning in office.

Reflection: Think of the awesome task of leading a nation with righteousness and justice. If you held high political office, how would you seek to do God's will? What is the relationship between political power and stewardship?

Prayer: Pray for the leaders of your country. Ask God's inspiration and guidance for all who work for the good of the community: social workers, garbage collectors, teachers, farmers, scientists . . . and yourself.

Psalm 73

"When my thoughts were bitter"

Introduction: As long as we are human, we will struggle, like Job, with the question of good and evil. Why do the wicked appear to prosper? Why do the righteous seem to suffer so much? The author of this psalm finds the answer in an experience of worship in the Temple. At such times we are confronted with the fact that while the "wicked" seem to be proud, we also pride ourselves because of our suffering. When we begin to regain our perspective, we can understand that the those who are less than pious are not immune to God's judgment. We also begin to understand the folly of our own self-pity.

Preparation: When you have centered yourself and are ready for prayer, ask God to help you to expose your jealousy of others and to recognize your own follies.

Read Psalm 73: Read the psalm through carefully, paying attention to the shifting emotions of the author. Then read it a second time to see where the critical turning point is for *you*.

Reflection: How do you feel about those who seem to glide through life without God and without a value system that respects others? Do you sometimes feel that the righteous suffer, while others don't?

Prayer: Ask God to help you to be more clear about this age-old question. Give thanks for any insights you have gained from this psalm.

Psalm 74

"Why do you keep your hands behind you?"

Introduction: Scholars are divided over the date of Psalm 74, which is a communal lament over the destruction and dese-cration of the Temple. It is possible that it dates from the Babylonian destruction in 587 B.C.E., although others argue for a later date. Feeling that they have been abandoned by God, the people lament and cry out that "all our sacred symbols are gone." No words are spared in the liturgical effort to move God to action. "Remember the covenant you made with us," the people cry out. God's mighty deeds of the past are remembered as if to say, "you can't abandon us now." "Why do you keep your hands behind you?" they ask pleadingly.

Preparation: As you get ready to pray, be mindful that you stand in a tradition which goes back thousands of years.

Read Psalm 74:   Imagine the siege of Jerusalem and the resulting de-struction of the Temple where you have worshiped daily all your life. Read the psalm as if you were a participant in the original liturgy.

Reflection: Can you begin to imagine how the people of Jeru-salem must have felt to see in smoking ruins the very symbol of all that their covenant with God had stood for? Through it all they experienced only silence from God. How would you react? Yet, was God to blame for the destruction?

Prayer: Ask God for a larger view of history, including the ability to see the consequences of human relation-ships whether they be personal or international.

Psalm 75

"Condemning some and acquitting others"

Introduction: Psalm 75 may have been brought together from two or more sources. It is a national thanksgiving for God's judgment in favor of the nation. Verses 2-3 state that God determines the time of judgment when a crisis threatens the world. Verses 4-5 are a reminder that God not only chooses the time, but always judges in favor of the wronged party. Verses 6-8 assert that judgment comes from the God of Israel and no other source. The psalm closes with the community rejoicing in the peace that has come from the God of justice.

Preparation: Ask God to be present with you as you pray. Take several long, slow, deep breaths, remembering that God breathes you into being with the divine *ruach*.

Read Psalm 75: Read the psalm through, paying attention to its basic structure. Then after a few moments of quiet, read it again and listen for its message for you.

Reflection: How often do you find yourself pronouncing judgment on another person, group, or nation? When a person does something you strongly disapprove of, how do you feel about him or her? Is your impatience a form of judgment? How can your tendency to judge others be tempered with understanding and tolerance?

Prayer: Ask God to make you more aware of the judgments you make about other persons and groups.

Psalm 77

"All night long I lift my hands in prayer"

Introduction: While this psalm would appear to be an individual lament, the "I" represents the anguish of the community of Israel when it seems that the Lord has forgotten the people. The problem of God's absence (verses 1-10) is resolved in the second half of the psalm by remembering the great deeds of the Lord in the exodus. Notice the repeated use of remember and meditate.

Preparation: As you prepare yourself to pray this psalm, you might recall a time in your life when you couldn't sleep because you kept thinking about something that was troubling you.

Read Psalm 77: Read the psalm, noticing the shift in its focus at verse 11. Read it a second time, letting yourself identify with some thought expressed in the psalm.

Reflection: Have you had the experience of lying awake all night worrying about something, feeling that God didn't care or wasn't there? Have you ever struggled with a problem for so long that it seemed that God had totally abandoned you? Are you helped by remembering the good times, when God seemed as close as your breathing?

Prayer: Converse with God about the feelings you have had while reflecting on the psalm.

Psalm 79

"O God, the heathen have invaded your land"

Introduction: Psalm 79 is a communal lament over the destruction of the Temple, probably reflecting the situation after the Babylonian invasion of 587 B.C.E. Jerusalem was devastated and bodies remained unburied in the streets. Israel was made the laughing stock of surrounding nations. The psalm interprets this event as a manifestation of God's anger with the people. Acknowledging their sin, the people ask God's forgiveness but still call for the punishment of the offending nations. This psalm is still prayed by Jews at the Western Wall of the Temple Mount on Friday afternoons.

Preparation: You have many things to do today, some of which can be done while thinking about something else. But prayer calls for your undivided attention. Take time to set aside other concerns in order to focus on your prayer.

Read Psalm 79: Read the psalm, imagining in your mind the destruction of Jerusalem and the Temple.

Reflection: If you have not read Psalm 78 recently, it will provide a good overview of Israel's salvation history, culminating with the building of the Temple. Against that background imagine the feeling of the people when the city and Temple were suddenly destroyed. The Jewish people have continued to suffer in the Diaspora, the Crusades, and the Holocaust.

Prayer: Let your prayer flow out of your reflection of Jewish suffering over the centuries.

Psalm 80

"You brought a grapevine out of Egypt"

Introduction: This communal lament seems to reflect a recent military defeat for the people of Israel. The psalm appeals to God as the "Shepherd of Israel" to come and save the "grapevine" brought out of Egypt and planted in Israel, which is now exposed and vulnerable to the nation's enemies. The people place their hope in God, promising never to turn away again. Verses 3, 7, and 19 are a repeated congregational refrain.

Preparation: Can you sit for five minutes and think of nothing? Can you sit for two minutes and think of one thing? Release yourself from distracting thoughts so that you can be fully open to the psalm.

Read Psalm 80: Read the psalm to become familiar with its content and imagery. After a few moments, read it again, as if you were part of a large congregation singing it together.

Reflection: Look again at the grapevine metaphor in the psalm. Reflect on the rich imagery of the vine being rooted in God with branches that extend everywhere, connecting all of God's people. Can you apply the image of the grapevine to today's "global village"?

Prayer: Let your prayer be a dialogue with God concerning the condition of the grapevine today.

Psalm 81

"Open your mouth, and I will feed you"

Introduction: It is possible that Psalm 81 is made up of two unrelated psalms reflected in verses 1-5 and 6-16. In the earlier section the community is called to praise God according to the law of Israel (verse 4). Then is recited a summary of the exodus, Israel's great act of liberation from Egypt. In verses 11-12 the people are reminded of their failure to obey the commands of God. This, combined with themes of both judgment and grace, gives the second part of the psalm a prophetic tone.

Preparation: Read the psalm carefully, noting the opening call to praise, followed by the prophetic retelling of the exodus story. Then take a few moments to quietly center yourself.

Read Psalm 81: Read the psalm again with appreciation for its thoughts.

Reflection: What idea or phrase struck you as you read this psalm? What basic elements of worship did you find in the psalm (praise, confession, instruction, dedication)? How do you respond to the words of God spoken in verses 6-16? What about the words, "Open your mouth, and I will feed you"? What is it in you that needs to be fed?

Prayer: In your prayer, ask God to help you know what it is in you that needs to be fed and how.

Psalm 82

"God presides in the heavenly council"

Introduction: In the ancient world it was commonly assumed that there were many gods with different degrees of influence and control over human affairs. This psalm boldly declares that the Lord is the only God. Other gods are false gods who do not uphold justice. These will be judged and defeated, leaving the Lord as the one true God who rules the nations.

Preparation: Before you begin to pray this psalm, ask yourself if you come to this experience out of habit, obligation, or out of a genuine desire to stand before God.

Read Psalm 82: Let your imagination help you read and pray this psalm. Begin with the opening verse, and set the scene as it suggests.

Reflection: What does the psalmist suggest are the differences between God and the gods? What does the psalm suggest as the marks of a true worshiper of God? Is the psalmist suggesting that certain powerful human beings are acting like gods?

Prayer: Pray that you may always be reminded of God's justice in specific ways, such as defending "the rights of the poor" and being "fair to the needy and the helpless."

Psalm 84

"One day spent in your Temple"

Introduction: In ancient times this psalm may have been used as a hymn sung by pilgrims on their way to visit Jerusalem and the Temple. Or it may have been the reflection of one who had been at the Temple and longed to return there. (Those who have visited Jerusalem in modern times have the same feeling, having sensed even the holiness of the site where the Temple once stood!) In either case it is a joyous psalm on what it is like to be in the presence of the Lord.

Preparation: Prepare yourself for meditation in a quiet place. Relax; imagine that you are about to make a once-in-a-lifetime pilgrimage to a holy place.

Read Psalm 84: Let it be your own personal hymn, expressing your desire to experience the presence of God.

Reflection: What would it be like for you to visit one of the great cathedrals of Europe, to sit quietly in prayer? Do you remember a place, perhaps outdoors, where you experienced the presence of God? What does this psalm say about God's relationship with you?

Prayer: Give thanks to God for your experience in prayer; for being reminded about holy places; for the yearning inside you to be in God's presence. Ask God to be present to you in other ways.

Psalm 85

"Bring us back, O God"

Introduction: Psalm 85 has been described both as a lament and as a prophetic liturgy. It is divided into three parts: Verses 1-3 remind about the Lord's past goodness to Israel; verses 4-7 are an urgent plea that the Lord might again save the people; and verses 8-13 offer the reassurance that the Lord will indeed deliver the people. The beauty and diction of the latter section are almost without parallel anywhere in the Psalter.

Preparation: Center yourself by releasing the tension that goes almost unnoticed in your body. Take several deep breaths. Ask God to be present in your meditation.

Read Psalm 85: Try reading this psalm out loud.

Reflection: What does the psalmist say about God's relationship with the people in the past? How do you feel about the petition for God to "bring us back"? What are some things in your life or in our national life which result in our need to be brought back to God? How do you feel about the faith of the psalmist as expressed in the closing section?

Prayer: In an easy conversational way, let your prayer flow out of your own reflection and feelings about this psalm.

Psalm 86

"I call to you in times of trouble"

Introduction: Psalm 86 has the characteristics of a lament, but it is otherwise difficult to describe. While it has all the marks of being the prayer of an individual, some feel that it was meant to be the plea of a nation. The psalm may have been pieced together with lines borrowed from other psalms, resulting in numerous reasons for the psalmist calling upon God. One scholar has suggested that the sense would be better and the structure more typical of a lament if the order were changed to verses 1-7, verses 14-17, then verses 8-13.

Preparation: If you have difficulty centering, you might want to think about the time of day when you pray. A full stomach is not conducive to meditation. Caffeine is also a problem for many people. You might want to experiment with different times.

Read Psalm 86: Try reading this psalm in the order suggested above.

Reflection: The psalm says, "I call to you in times of trouble." Is that enough? What about when things are going well? Why do *you* pray? Which of the reasons for prayer given in this psalm feels most right to you?

Prayer: Share some of your feelings about prayer with God. Feel free to ask questions.

Psalm 87

"The Lord . . . will include them all"

Introduction: Psalm 87 is difficult to date, difficult to interpret, and difficult to understand from the point of view of the text. It may date to the time of the exile or it may be later. We don't know to whom it is addressed. The exiles are one possibility; the Jews of the Diaspora are another. One thing is certain. It reaches out to all nations with the generosity of Second Isaiah. One scholar suggests that the order of the verses should be: 1, 2, 3, 6, 4, 5, 7.

Preparation: Has your pattern of prayer become too routine? If so, you may want to consider changing something or adding something to your ritual. Above all, make sure that this is a special time set apart from other activities of the day.

Read Psalm 87: Read the psalm slowly, using the order of verses suggested above.

Reflection: How wonderful it would be if Jerusalem today could be a truly international city, free of political struggle. What would it be like to have such a place where people of all nations could come to worship and celebrate together?

Prayer: Pray for all nations and peoples; pray for the leaders of nations; pray that God will make the nations strong, not in weapons, but in faith.

Psalm 88

"I am close to death"

Introduction: This is a very personal lament on the part of someone who is sick and near death. It may be that the disease was leprosy. As a lament, this psalm is unusual in that it does not end with a note of hope and praise. There may be slight hope implied in the questions found in verses 10-12 and in the very fact that the sick person is praying for help. It may be that this is the most somber lament in the entire Psalter.

Preparation: Christians have often used meditations on death as a means of enhancing personal humility. It is a somber reminder that we must finally let go of everything. Can you temporarily let go of everything to be with God in these moments?

Read Psalm 88: Read the psalm first to familiarize yourself with its flow and content. Then read it again, trying to feel the emotion of the author.

Reflection: What would it be like to be "like the slain lying in their graves" and yet still reflect on the meaning of death and pray for God's help? What is behind the psalmist's blaming God for the circumstances? What clever arguments does the author make in verses 10-11? Have you known persons very near to death or been there yourself? How do you feel about your own eventual death? What are your greatest fears? Do you feel an assurance of God's care even beyond death?

Prayer: Share with God your feelings about death. Explore them, asking for greater understanding and insight.

Psalm 90

"Teach us how short our life is"

Introduction: Psalm 90 is one of the most personal of the Psalms. It could well be called the psalm for those who are "middle-aged" because its theme has to do with the shortness of life and the need for wisdom as we grow older. It may be that Psalm 90 is a combination of two earlier prayers: verses 1-12, which are more pessimistic; and verses 13-17, which reflect a growing maturity and hope for a greater vision of life.

Preparation: Sit quietly for several minutes, allowing the thoughts and cares that fill your mind to drift away, like smoke rising gently from a campfire. Enjoy the silence. Discover that silence is not empty, but filled with potential.

Read Psalm 90: Think about your own life as you read this psalm.

Reflection: How often do you lament how rapidly life seems to pass? Do you wish you had done more with the time and opportunities you had in the past? Do you wish for more "quality" in the time you have left?

Prayer: Share your feelings in an informal conversational way with God. Listen. Pray with the psalmist, "Fill us each morning with your constant love."

Psalm 91

"God will put . . . angels in charge of you"

Introduction: This song of trust and confidence, often used in the
office of compline, may have been written by one who
has come as a pilgrim to the Temple and is now about
to return home. Verses 3-13 are promises that God's
protection, felt so strongly in the Temple, will always
be available for those who make the Lord their refuge.
In verses 14-16 the protection of God is promised
directly to those who maintain their trust, even in
danger. "He will cover you with his wings" refers to
the winged creatures which guarded the ark in the
Temple (see 1 Kings 6:23-28). In their accounts of
Jesus' temptation, both Luke and Matthew quote verses 11-12 of this psalm.

Preparation: Imagine yourself nearing the end of a visit to your
favorite church or cathedral, where you have felt the
security of God's protection. Prepare yourself for a
final prayer before leaving for home.

Read Psalm 91: Read the psalm, hearing the promises God makes to
those who come to the Lord for safety. Let God's
promises in verses 14-16 be addressed to you personally.

Reflection: St. Antony of the Desert said: "When you are alone,
know that there is with you an angel assigned by
God." Does this mean that even if something unfortu-
nate should happen to us, God is still with us?

Prayer: Go back and read those phrases which were most
vivid for you, letting them begin your prayer.

Psalm 92

"Like trees . . . that still bear fruit in old age"

Introduction: Psalm 92 is a gentle hymn of thanksgiving, offering praise to God for "your constant love every morning and your faithfulness every night." There is a mature reflection on the folly of the wicked, who may "grow like weeds" but will ultimately be defeated. The righteous, on the other hand, are presented not as holier-than-thou, but humbly as those who "will flourish like . . . trees . . . that still bear fruit in old age and are always green and strong," all because of the justice of the Lord. There is a Jewish tradition that this psalm was sung by Adam on the first Sabbath of creation.

Preparation: Give yourself time to savor the gentle tone of this psalm.

Read Psalm 92: This psalm is worth reading through several times. Each of its four stanzas is capable of standing alone.

Reflection: Verses 1-4 speak of the simple joy of praying morning and evening. Is your praying joyful, or is it work? How do you feel about the rich imagery of trees in verses 12-14? Do you remember the image of trees in Psalm 1?

Prayer: Read each of the four stanzas again; then let your own responses be your prayer.

Psalm 93

"The earth is set firmly in place"

Introduction: Here is one of the Psalter's great hymns of praise. It celebrates the Lord as King of the universe. A storm involving the sea is often a symbol of suffering and anxiety. This psalm declares that the Creator's power overcomes and sets limits on the power of the sea. God thus makes the whole universe secure. Verses 1*b* and 5 serve to frame the rest of the psalm: "The earth is set firmly in place" and "Your laws are eternal."

Preparation: Perhaps you can recall a violent storm which you have experienced; then remember the calm after the storm. When you feel that calm inside yourself, sing with the psalmist this great hymn to God the Creator.

Read Psalm 93: You may want to read this brief psalm several times to better appreciate both its beauty and structure.

Reflection: Most of us have experienced the awesome power of a storm while we were secure indoors beside a glowing fire. Our lives are often like that, peaceful and secure, yet threatened by outside forces. When you are surrounded by turmoil in your life, can you also affirm that "the earth is set firmly in place" and that "the Lord rules supreme"?

Prayer: Pray that you might be able to affirm the power of God and feel totally secure even in those times when the storms of life are wild and terrifying.

Psalm 95

"Don't be stubborn, as your ancestors were"

Introduction: It is likely that Psalm 95 is the outline of a procession moving up to the Temple for worship. In verses 1-5 the congregation praises the Lord as it marches through the courtyards toward the Temple. In our terms verses 6-7a form a call to worship as they reach the Temple. At this point a priest reads from the scriptures and comments on their meaning. The theme comes from the Exodus tradition. *Massah* and *Meribah* are places whose names mean "testing" and "complaining" and recall that the Israelites tested and complained against the Lord in the desert (see Exodus 17:1-7). The sermon ends with a warning against those who are unfaithful to the commands of the Lord. (See also Hebrews 3:7-19 and 4:3-11.)

Preparation: When you are centered and ready to read the psalm, imagine yourself in a crowd of worshippers, processing to the Temple.

Read Psalm 95: Read verses 1-7a as a processional hymn of praise and a call to worship, then the remaining verses as a homily on the exodus tradition.

Reflection: Our spiritual ancestors were stubborn, complaining to Moses about the difficult conditions in the desert and asking, "Is the Lord with us or not?" Do you sometimes test God with your stubbornness?

Prayer: Admit your own stubbornness to God and ask for help in moving beyond it.

Psalm 96

"Praise the Lord's glorious name"

Introduction: The author of this psalm has drawn together themes from several sources, including Psalm 29 (compare verses 7-10 with Psalm 29:1-2). Originally this psalm helped readers recall God's care of the Israelites during the exodus, but it was later adapted for use in the celebration of the feast of tabernacles, especially at the Temple in Jerusalem. The invitation to "sing a new song" in verse 1 is reminiscent of the hope expressed in Isaiah 42:10. A second invitation (verses 7-10) calls on worshipers to bring their gifts to God in the Temple. The final section, verses 11-13, invites all of creation to join in greeting the creator God.

Preparation: Before you pray this psalm, quiet the many voices in your mind and prepare yourself for unrestrained joy in celebration of the creation by God.

Read Psalm 96: As the opening words suggest, this psalm is so full of joy that it needs to be sung, rather than read! Sing it in your own way.

Reflection: What reasons are given in the psalm for singing "a new song to the Lord"? If you have access to one of those breathtaking photographs of the earth taken from space, look at it as you reflect on the meaning of this psalm.

Prayer: Use your own words and images to "sing a new song to the Lord" as you celebrate all that God has done.

Psalm 97

"With righteousness and justice"

Introduction: Psalms 93 and 95-100 all proclaim that the Lord is King. The Lord's greatest act was that of creation. In Psalm 97, the Lord is surrounded by clouds, darkness, fire, and lightning, images drawn from the Mount Sinai tradition. The appearance of God brings shame to those who worship idols. The first eight verses represent the Lord's manifestation to the world at large; then in verses 9-12 the Lord is made known to his people Israel. Both sections begin (verses 1 and 8) with gladness and rejoicing.

verse 1:	The Lord is king;
verses 2-6:	The epiphany or manifestation of the Lord;
verses 7-8:	The result of the Lord's manifestation;
verses 9-11:	The great mercy and love of the Lord;
verse 12:	A call for the people to respond thankfully.

Preparation: Open yourself to reflect on the great power and mystery of God.

Read Psalm 97: Read the psalm to get a sense of its structure outlined above. Then read it again to hear what it says to you.

Reflection: How do you see the power and righteousness of God in the psalm? What other images would you use to describe God's power in the world?

Prayer: Offer your prayer to God based on your feelings in response to the psalm.

Psalm 98

"O sing to the Lord a new song" (NRSV)

Introduction: This psalm was used in the Temple liturgy in celebration of God's renewal of creation. All of creation is included, and the sea (verse 7) is part of the musical ensemble giving praise to the Lord. The psalm is influenced by Isaiah 40–55, and by Psalm 96. Psalm 98 helps us recall Israel's release from captivity in Babylon and from all other forms of oppression. It proclaims that God's judgment is a vindication of those who have been oppressed.

Preparation: As you quiet your otherwise anxious spirit, know that you are preparing for an experience of complete joy and celebration.

Read Psalm 98: Imagine this psalm being sung to the sound of festive trumpets as you read it.

Reflection: The psalm celebrates God as King, a concept which may sound unnatural to our modern democratic ears. It may be helpful to remember that Israel itself had a king for only about one-third of its history, a 1,300-year period extending from the Exodus until A.D. 70.

Prayer: Give thanks to God for a larger perspective on history, extending all the way back to the exodus. Celebrate God's continuing victory over oppression.

Psalm 99

"A God who forgives"

Introduction: This is another of the psalms that celebrate the Lord as King. The emphasis here is on the Lord's special relationship with Israel. Zion is the place where the supreme power of God is visible, and it is the people of Israel who have maintained the historic relationship. God has established justice and righteousness in Israel. The Exodus tradition is recalled in verses 6-7. The Lord is a God who forgives, "even though you punished them for their sins." The call to offer praise to God is repeated in verses 5 and 9.

Preparation: This psalm calls upon us to give praise simply because God is God. That is enough reason for prayer!

Read Psalm 99: Read this psalm, remembering that those who wrote it were *your* spiritual ancestors and that in the communion of the saints you pray it also with them.

Reflection: Without looking back at the psalm for a moment, recall some of the reasons given for our praising God. What reasons can you add for giving praise to God? How do you feel about the relationship of forgiveness and punishment (verse 8)?

Prayer: As you pray, stand with your spiritual ancestors and allow them to be present in your prayer.

Psalm 100

"God made us and to God we belong" (AP)

Introduction: Here is a psalm probably second in popularity only to Psalm 23. It is well known because of the hymn, "All People That on Earth Do Dwell." It was sung by worshipers as they entered the gate of the Temple and passed into its courts. Contained in it are six simple statements which together form a creed of the Jewish faith:
1) The Lord is our God;
2) God is our creator;
3) We are God's people;
4) The Lord is good;
5) God's love is eternal;
6) God's faithfulness is forever.

Preparation: Empty your mind of the clutter of the day and prepare to immerse yourself in the simple beauty of this psalm!

Read Psalm 100: Read the psalm very slowly, pausing after each verse. Read it again or read the words of the hymn: "All People That on Earth Do Dwell."

Reflection: Go back to the psalm again and take a few moments to reflect on each verse.

Prayer: What line of the psalm remains in your mind? Let your response to that line be the start of your prayer.

Psalm 103

"God knows what we are made of" (AP)

Introduction: Some of the psalms, like 8, 29 and 104, hold up life, its beauty and goodness, as a mirror to God. Such is reason enough to praise God. But Psalm 103 takes us even deeper, reminding us of God's compassion toward us in our weakness and guilt. It is a reminder that God's love is *unconditional* and completely dependable. It is there even when we least expect or deserve it, which has caused some to refer to it as God's "most amazing grace."

Preparation: Part of entering into the silence of God is learning how to relax the tensions of both mind and body. Take a few minutes to be aware of such tensions, and then let them go.

Read Psalm 103: Make this your personal prayer as you read it.

Reflection: Most of us have experienced the power of being forgiven and the power of loving someone who might not deserve it at the moment. The psalmist proclaims that God's love is unconditional. God "does not punish us as we deserve."

Prayer: Ask God to help you to grow in your ability to love unconditionally.

Psalm 104

"When vou give them breath, they are created"

Introduction: Psalm 104 has been called "the gem of the Psalter." It is a joyful hymn celebrating God's creation of the world. As such, it is reminiscent of the Genesis account in which God turns the chaotic forces of water and darkness into integral parts of the created world. God's life-giving breath is in everything: "When you give them breath, they are created." In this psalm one even has a sense of the ecological interdependence of all of God's creation.

Preparation: You might want to allow extra time for the praying of this psalm, not just because it is a bit longer, but because its imagery is so very rich.

Read Psalm 104: Read the psalm slowly, allowing yourself time to see in your mind the images called forth. Then take the time to go back and read it a second time with even greater care, allowing it to "sing" itself as you read it.

Reflection: Does this psalm make you want to go back and read the creation stories in Genesis 1 and 2? If so, do it! Then read the psalm again. What are the implications of this psalm for our stewardship of creation?

Prayer: Give God praise for the wonder of creation; ask for greater insight into the meaning of our having dominion over the earth. Ask what you might be able to do to help.

Psalm 105

"God remembered the sacred promise to Abraham" (AP)

Introduction:	The first fifteen verses of this psalm come from 1 Chronicles 16:8-22. It is a hymn to the Lord who made a covenant with Abraham and continued to guide the people through their experience in Egypt, during the exodus, and finally into the promised land of Canaan.

verses 1-6:	Israel is invited to praise the Lord;
verses 7-11:	God will keep the promise made to Abraham;
verses 12-15:	Ancestors in Canaan;
verses 16-22:	Joseph in Egypt;
verses 23-38:	Israel in Egypt;
verses 39-45:	Israel led out of Egypt back to Canaan.

Preparation:	As you look forward to praying this psalm, remember that you are part of an ancient tradition that we moderns tend to forget.
Read Psalm 105:	Read the psalm carefully, being aware of its overview of the history of God's people Israel. Read it a second time, looking for phrases that address you in a special way.
Reflection:	How do you respond to this retelling of the history of Israel? How do you see the role of God in history in more recent times?
Prayer:	Let your prayer begin with the images and phrases that you found especially meaningful in the psalm.

Psalm 106

"We have sinned as our ancestors did"

Introduction: In modern terms we might call Psalm 106 a prayer of confession. The opening verses speak of God's goodness and call upon God to help. Immediately following is a long series of laments recalling, among other things, the exodus experience of the Israelites. Many examples are given of God's saving power in spite of the unfaithfulness of the people. The psalm closes with a call for God to "bring us back."

Preparation: Centering prayer enables the mind to concentrate on *one* thing, rather than many things. Use whatever method seems best for you to prepare yourself to pray this psalm.

Read Psalm 106: Read the psalm as a part of *your* own history, remembering all those times when God rescued *your* people.

Reflection: In the Psalms there is a strong sense of remembering our story. Events of the past such as the exodus and the Babylonian exile are remembered almost as if the current generation had participated in them. Christians can be instructed by remembering our history. We have much to learn from the sins of our past such as slavery, the use of the atomic bomb in World War II, our treatment of Native American people, and the internment of American citizens of Japanese descent during World War II.

Prayer: Ask God's forgiveness for the sins of your own people.

Psalm 107

"Let them thank the Lord for constant love" (AP)

Introduction: In ancient Near Eastern thought the number four represented totality. Drawing on images of the exodus and return from captivity, Psalm 107 speaks of God bringing the people back from the four corners of the earth. Verses 4-32 help us remember four groups saved by God: 1) those who wandered in the desert; 2) those who were in prison; 3) those who were sick; and 4) those in perilous seas. Each of these sections follows this pattern: danger, prayer, deliverance, and exhortation to thank the Lord. The style changes in the final verses, but the theme of God's rescue and care for the people continues.

Preparation: If you find yourself having difficulty clearing your mind for praying the scriptures, you are not alone. Try not to be frustrated with all the thoughts that flood your consciousness. Simply dismiss them and continue.

Read Psalm 107: Read the psalm slowly to gain a sense of its content. Then go back and read it a second time, noting the introduction (verses 1-3); the four sections beginning with verses 4, 10, 17, and 23; and the closing reflection (verses 33-43).

Reflection: Note the words of the introduction: "[God] has rescued *you* from your enemies and has brought *you* back from foreign countries" (italics mine). Perhaps you were wandering in some spiritual desert. Perhaps you were imprisoned by something in your life. Perhaps you were ill.

Prayer: Thank the Lord for constant love.

Psalm 109

"They tell lies about me"

Introduction:	Psalm 109 is a challenge for those who pray the psalms. Verses 6 through 19 are totally vindictive, reflecting a blind, unforgiving anger. This section represents the invocation of a curse on some enemy. Yet, this vindictiveness is set in the context of an otherwise pious prayer, indeed, pious to the point of self-righteousness! It ends (verses 30-31) on a note of trust and confidence that God will be faithful.
Preparation:	Take time to convert your *empty* silence into a *full* silence . . . your *anxious* silence into a *peaceful* silence . . . your *restless* silence into a *restful* silence.
Read Psalm 109:	Read the psalm, trying to *feel* what the author might have felt.
Reflection:	Have you ever felt like the author of this psalm? There is truth in the observation that when we are angry about something, we often take it out on others. It is not surprising then, that the anger and self-pity of the psalmist is expressed in such self-righteousness. What can your anger teach you about yourself?
Prayer:	Ask God to help you express your anger in a constructive way, a way which leaves the door open for compassion and reconciliation.

Psalm 111

"The way to become wise is to honor the Lord"

Introduction: Psalm 111 is another acrostic with each verse beginning with a successive letter of the Hebrew alphabet.
We are presented with a list of spiritual insights into
the ways of God. Verses 1-2 are an introduction;
verses 3-9 speak of God's righteousness, power, faithfulness, and justice, leading up to God's covenant
relationship with the people in verse 9. The con-
clusion comes in verse 10, "The way to become wise is
to honor the Lord."

Preparation: For many people, posture is an important part of
centering prayer. If you have difficulty centering, you
might try another position, such as sitting erect in a
chair with your back straight and your head balanced.

Read Psalm 111: Read the psalm once aloud to discover its simplicity
and content. Then after a moment or two of reflec-
tion, go back and read it a second time.

Reflection: Try reflecting on each of the ten verses of the psalm.
Prior to reading this psalm, how would you have said
that a person becomes wise?

Prayer: Ask God to help you make your faith as simple and
direct as this psalm.

Psalm 112

"Happy is the person who is generous"

Introduction: This psalm is written in the same acrostic style as Psalm 111 and may have been written by the same person. It extols the rewards which come to those who are generous. Such rewards include an abundance of descendants, prosperity in this life, and a good conscience. In the closing verse a stark contrast is drawn between those who are generous and the wicked. We are given a choice . . . and a response is expected! (Compare with Psalms 1 and 15.)

Preparation: Few things in contemporary life arouse stronger feelings in us than money. This may be a good psalm to pray when you are in the midst of paying your monthly bills or reworking your personal budget!

Read Psalm 112: As usual, read the psalm at least twice. During the second reading, be sure to take plenty of time to savor and reflect on every verse.

Reflection: How do you react to the connection the psalmist makes between happiness and one's attitude toward wealth? Place equal amounts of money in both of your hands. Make a tight fist with one hand; keep the other hand open and extended before you. How do you feel about the contrast? How do you feel about the expression: "It's only money"?

Prayer: Allow your reflections and feelings to initiate your prayer.

Psalm 113

"[God] raises the poor from the dust"

Introduction: Psalm 113 is the first of the six great *Hallel* (meaning "song of praise") psalms, which were sung at the Passover celebration. It opens with a call for the name of the Lord to be praised by "the servants of the Lord" (worshipers or choir members). The name of the Lord is praised everywhere (verses 2-3) because the Lord "rules over all nations." The last three verses refer to the Lord's justice, which in the Bible means not just to render a verdict, but to actively right wrongs. Thus the poor are lifted from the dust, the needy are raised from their misery, and the childless wife is given children. The psalm is a reminder that no human problem is beyond God's healing.

Preparation: This great hymn of praise not only calls forth joy, but has the joyful praise of God as its very reason for being! Prepare yourself to pray it joyfully.

Read Psalm 113: As you read this psalm, imagine it being sung antiphonally by a priest and congregation.

Reflection: Compare the active justice and mercy of God recognized in this psalm with Mary's song of praise in Luke 1:51-55.

Prayer: Offer your prayer with great joy, and at the same time pray for God's justice to be present to the poor and needy where you are.

Psalm 114

"Tremble, O earth, at the presence of the Lord" (NRSV)

Introduction: Once again, exodus (the Easter event of the Jewish faith) is the focus. Few if any of the psalms can match the literary form, dramatic action, parallelism, and brevity of Psalm 114. The waters of the Red Sea and the Jordan River gave way as the Lord led the Israelites to their promised land. Even the mountains and hills cooperated. This psalm accompanied processions in the Temple as the people recalled the events of the exodus. It is one of the *Hallel* (praise) psalms (113-118) used during the celebration of Passover.

Preparation: As you prepare yourself to pray this psalm, ask God to open your spirit to offer praise as you recall the powerful events our spiritual ancestors witnessed in the exodus.

Read Psalm 114: This psalm is so brief and so well written that it almost sings itself. Allow it to sing as you read it.

Reflection: Take time to remember the events of the exodus which are recalled in the psalm. Whether or not you choose to believe such events physically took place, remember that they represent unusual things which really did happen spiritually to God's people.

Prayer: Give thanks to God for the rich tradition in which we are invited to participate.

Psalm 115

"Their gods are made of silver and gold"

Introduction: Some feel that this psalm came out of the experience of the exile, helping the people to maintain faith in the Lord while they were surrounded by pagan gods. Others suggest that it came out of a period when Israel was weak and experienced the taunts of pagan neighbors. It opens with a sharp contrast drawn between the Lord and the false gods of others (verses 1-8). The next three verses were sung responsively by priest and people. The blessing in verses 12-15 was said by the priest alone. The closing verses were then sung by the entire congregation.

Preparation: Take whatever time is necessary to quiet the commotion of your mind, your spirit, and your body.

Read Psalm 115: Read the psalm; then pray the psalm.

Reflection: Some people make gods of silver and gold. Others make gods of things like television, cars, success, or fame. What and where are your gods? What gods have you made? How have you become like them?

Prayer: To whom do you address your prayer? Ask for help in distinguishing between the God who created you and the gods you have created.

Psalm 116

"I was filled with fear and anxiety"

Introduction: While this psalm was used in congregational worship, its theme and content are very personal. It is the thanksgiving of an individual who, having been spared from death during a serious illness, comes to the courtyard of the Temple to make a thank offering to God and to fulfill promises made to God during the course of the illness. It shows a spirit of sincere devotion enhanced by deep gratitude for the mercies received.

Preparation: Sometimes we come to prayer with such intense feelings (anger, anxiety, etc.) that we cannot center ourselves. Try asking God to help you let go of these feelings temporarily. You can return to them later and deal with them more constructively.

Read Psalm 116: Read the psalm, being aware of any feelings expressed by the psalmist which you have experienced in your own life.

Reflection: Have you experienced some of these feelings in your own life:
- "The danger of death was all around me."
- "I was filled with fear and anxiety."
- "I am completely crushed."
- "No one can be trusted."

Prayer: Ask God to help you accept the reality of such feelings and to help you to see a larger perspective beyond them.

Psalm 117

"Praise the Lord, all nations!"

Introduction: It seems unlikely that this shortest of all psalms was originally an independent composition. Nor can we be certain that it is a fragment belonging to another psalm. At first glance it seems to represent a universal point of view calling upon "all nations" and "all peoples" to praise the Lord. The next verse speaks of God's love for *us* (meaning the Israelites) and of God's "faithfulness," both concepts used in the psalms only in reference to Israel, never for foreigners. The result is a theological view which some would call evangelistic or sectarian.

Preparation: Most of us make at least a minimal effort to care for our bodies and our emotional health. Is our spiritual health and growth any less important?

Read Psalm 117: Read the psalm aloud.

Reflection: While many of us are shy about sharing our faith, we affirm the value of doing so. We want others to know about God's love, especially those whose lives have not been touched by faith. At the same time many of us have had the experience of being approached by others whose evangelistic zeal causes them to be self-righteous and judgmental. Where do we find a balance between witness and triumphalism?

Prayer: Ask God to help you be a witness to your faith and still be respectful of the faith of others.

Psalm 119

Introduction: Psalm 119 is not only the longest of the Psalms, but also the most structured, at least at first glance. It contains twenty-two stanzas, one for each of the twenty-two letters of the Hebrew alphabet. Furthermore, each stanza contains eight verses, each of which begins with the same letter of the alphabet.

The general theme of the psalm is the law of God. However, the idea of law is to be broadly interpreted. It does not mean "law" in the sense of the classical Roman *lex*, the basis of our western legal system. Perhaps it would be better to use the word *teaching* instead of *law*. As Carroll Stuhlmueller has said:

> It is a way of life, learned and integrated by the law of Moses but not identifiable with it; it is a keen sensitivity to oral traditions as these transmit ideals, the sorrows, and the struggles of Israel's ordinary folk; it is personal dedication to what one perceives to be the best, not just conformity to a legal code; it is not searching the past but living in the present moment where God is to be found and where ancient traditions take on a new vitality; it is satisfaction even within monotonous daily life, not with a frenetic drive for excitement and wondrous deeds; most of all . . . it is seeking God with one's whole heart. . . . [6]

This understanding of law is affirmed in most biblical translations by the use of a variety of synonyms, each of which points in the direction of the meaning of the original Hebrew. These synonyms include *commandments, statutes, word, instructions, judgments, teachings, truths, precepts, ordinances, rulings, decrees.*

We are reminded of the image in Psalm 1, that those who "find joy in obeying the Law of the Lord . . . are like trees that grow beside a stream." The author of this psalm was one who thrived on God's teaching and was perhaps very familiar with the second part of Psalm 19.

Verse 164 of this psalm is the source of the monastic practice of seven prayer offices each day. Verses 55, 62, and 147 may well have been the inspiration of the night office. They serve also to remind us that the biblical injunction to "pray continually" extends even to our sleep . . . and to our sleepless nights.

The psalm is set solidly in the first person, reflecting individual rather than a community form of piety. As such, its many verses often convey the feeling of a private prayer journal. Each stanza is an invitation to our personal meditation.

Because of its unusual length and structure we will approach our praying of this psalm in a slightly different manner. The present introduction will serve as an introduction to the entire psalm. Each stanza will be the focus of a separate meditation and is preceded by a brief quotation which is related to the theme verse.

Psalm 119:1-8

"How I hope that I shall be faithful"

The road to self-knowledge does not pass through faith. But only through the self-knowledge we gain by pursuing the fleeting light in the depth of our being do we reach the point where we can grasp what faith is. How many have been driven into outer darkness by empty talk about faith as something to be rationally comprehended, something "true."[7]

—DAG HAMMARSKJÖLD

Preparation: As you ready yourself to pray this psalm, take a moment to call to mind some of the great people of faith in the Bible.

Read Psalm 119: (1-8) Read this stanza slowly; try to get a sense of the feeling of the psalmist.

Reflection: What does it mean to you to "have faith"? What does it mean to "be faithful"? What is the relationship between faithfulness and obeying God's law? How have you struggled with faithfulness in your life? What advice does the psalmist give about being faithful?

Prayer: Let these eight verses be *your* prayer for faithfulness.

Psalm 119:9-16

"I treasure your word in my heart" (NRSV)

To pray is to descend with the mind into the heart, and there to stand before the face of the Lord, ever-present, all seeing, within you.[8]

—THEOPHAN THE RECLUSE

Prayer is standing in the presence of God with the mind in the heart; that is, at that point of our being where there are no divisions or distinctions and where we are totally one. There God's Spirit dwells and there the great encounter takes place. There heart speaks to heart, because there we stand before the face of the Lord, all-seeing, within us.[9]

—HENRI J.M. NOUWEN

Preparation:	As you prepare to pray these verses, try to be aware of what it is within you that desires to pray.
Read Psalm 119: (9-16)	Read the verses several times, slowly, trying to distinguish between the thoughts and feelings of the psalmist.
Reflection:	Just why is it that you want to pray? Is it because your mind says it is a good thing to do? Or does your heart yearn for God, "as a deer longs for a stream of cool water" (Psalm 42)? Do you "take pleasure" in God's laws? If so, do you do so with your head or with your heart?
Prayer:	Try to pray this psalm with your heart.

Psalm 119:17-24

"Open my eyes, so that I may see . . . "

Corpus Christi

Yea, I have understood
How all things are one great oblation made:
He on our altars, we on the world's rood.
Even as this corn,
Earth-born,
We are snatched from the sod;
Reaped, ground to grist,
Crushed and tormented in the Mills of God,
And offered at Life's hands, a living Eucharist.[10]

—EVELYN UNDERHILL

Preparation: As you prepare to pray this section, pray that your own eyes may be opened to new truth.

Read Psalm 119: Read these verses reflectively, at least twice.
(17-24)

Reflection: How often have you read a biblical passage or heard a sermon in which you had a fleeting glimpse of a much larger truth? Perhaps that is the feeling behind this passage. Can you pray with the psalmist to have your eyes opened, to know God's judgments, to see "the wonderful truths" in God's teachings? And even though you may not *fully* understand, can you affirm in faith the truth you now see partially?

Prayer: Pray with the psalmist to have *your* eyes opened.

Psalm 119:25-32

"I lie defeated in the dust"

To be in a state of depression is. . . . to be unable to occupy yourself with anything much except your state of depression. Even the most marvelous thing is like music to the deaf. Even the greatest thing is like a shower of stars to the blind. You do not raise either your heart or your eyes to the heights because to do so only reminds you that you are yourself in the depths. Even if, like the Psalmist, you are inclined to cry out "O LORD," it is a cry like Jonah's from the belly of the whale.[11]

—FREDERICK BUECHNER

Preparation: Can you remember a time when you were depressed, unable to see beyond the gloom in your life?

Read Psalm 119: (25-32) Can you feel what the author of these verses felt?

Reflection: Have you ever felt "defeated in the dust" or "overcome by sorrow"? If so, you know that things which look wonderful to those around you do not look at all wonderful to you. In such times, we have to open ourselves to the advice and care of others, knowing that in all likelihood they are seeing things in a much better perspective. At the same time we continue to pray, as the psalmist does, for understanding, guidance, and strength.

Prayer: Pray for greater understanding of depression.

Psalm 119:33-40

"Give me the desire to obey your laws rather than to get rich"

For the white man each blade of grass or spring of water has a price tag on it. . . . And the prairie becomes a thing without life—no more prairie dogs, no more badgers, foxes, coyotes. The big birds of prey used to feed on prairie dogs, too. So you hardly see an eagle these days. The bald eagle is your symbol. You see him on your money, but your money is killing him. When a people start killing off their own symbols they are in a bad way.[12]

—JOHN FIRE/LAME DEER

Preparation: Before you center yourself to pray this psalm, place your checkbook or some of your credit cards on a table in front of you.

Read Psalm 119: (33-40) What issues is the psalmist struggling with?

Reflection: Can you think of other scripture passages which indicate a contradiction between following God's teaching and seeking wealth? Have you experienced such a conflict in your own life? What compromises have you made with God's teaching in order to maintain your present lifestyle?

Prayer: Pray for insight into your own struggle with money and with loving and living according to God's teaching.

Psalm 119:41-48

"I will live in perfect freedom"

> By all means they try to hold me secure
> who love me in this world.
> But it is otherwise with thy love
> which is greater than theirs, and thou keepest me free.
> Lest I forget them they never venture to leave me alone.
> But day passes by after day and thou are not seen.
> If I call not thee in my prayers, if I keep not thee in my
> heart, thy love for me still waits for my love.[13]
>
> —RABINDRANATH TAGORE

Preparation:	Reflect a moment on what freedom means to you. Then quiet yourself to pray this psalm.
Read Psalm 119: (41-48)	Read this stanza two or three times.
Reflection:	What does freedom mean for the psalmist? How does living God's word bring freedom? How is God a source of freedom in Tagore's poem? Will you remember this kind of freedom sometime in the future when God seems to be absent from you?
Prayer:	Enter into a dialogue with God about how much freedom you need and how much you want.

Psalm 119:49-56

"Even in my suffering I was comforted"

The soul knows well and feels that love is not found in the labors and sufferings of those in whom it rules, but that all who want to attain to love must seek it in fear and pursue it in faith, exercising themselves in longing, not sparing themselves in great labors, in many sufferings, underdoing many sorrows and enduring much contempt. The soul must not despise these things: small though they be, they must seem great, until it attains to the state where love rules in it and performs its own mighty works, making great things small, labor easy, suffering sweet, and all debts paid.[14]

—BEATRICE OF NAZARETH

Preparation: As you ready yourself for the praying of these verses of Psalm 119, call to mind a time in your life when you struggled with suffering.

Read Psalm 119: Read these verses several times to understand the
(49-56) inner feelings of the psalmist.

Reflection: Have you experienced the special comfort of God which comes to those who suffer? What do you think about the statement that "undeserved suffering is redemptive"? What is the difference between those who find comfort in suffering and those who "enjoy" their suffering?

Prayer: Give thanks to God for the gifts which come through suffering and for the grace to receive those gifts.

Psalm 119:57-64

"I have considered my conduct"

In our heart we come to see ourselves as sinners embraced by the mercy of God. It is this vision that makes us cry out, "Lord Jesus Christ, Son of the living God, have mercy on me, a sinner." The prayer of the heart challenges us to hide absolutely nothing from God and to surrender ourselves unconditionally to [God's] mercy.[15]

—HENRI J.M. NOUWEN

Preparation: As you pray these verses, open yourself completely to God, asking for the grace to be fully honest.

Read Psalm 119: Read these verses at least twice. Notice the different
(57-64) themes that emerge.

Reflection: What things struck you in these verses? What is the relationship between considering one's own conduct and the desire to obey God's commands? Have you taken time lately to consider your own conduct . . . as others might consider it? In such a perspective, we all live by God's mercy.

Prayer: Pray for the courage to consider your own conduct in different situations and relationships. Ask for God's mercy and for God's help in obedience.

Psalm 119:65-72

"It is good for me that I was humbled" (NRSV)

Repentance is not a mere feeling of sorrow or contrition for an act of wrongdoing. The regret I feel when I act impatiently or speak crossly is not repentance. 'Contrition without repentance is a feeder of pride.' Repentance is contrition for what we are in our fundamental beings, that we are wrong in our deepest roots because our interior government is by Self and not by God.

And it is an activity of the whole person. Unless I will to be different the mind will not follow.

True repentance brings an urge to be different, because of the sense of the incessant movement of what I am, forming forming, forming, what I shall be in the years to come.[16]

—FLORENCE ALLSHORN

Preparation: Get in touch with your own need to repent before you pray this psalm.

Read Psalm 119: Read these eight verses to hear what the author is
(65-72) saying; then read them again asking what they say for you.

Reflection: What does "repentance" mean for you? How is repentance more than contrition? How strong is your own "urge to be different"? What would you have to do in order to be different? Can you resolve to take a first step in that direction?

Prayer: Ask God to grant you true repentance.

Psalm 119:73-80

" . . . Because I trust in your promise"

Abram had a vision and heard the Lord say to him, "Do not be afraid, Abram. I will shield you from danger and give you a great reward."

But Abram answered, "Sovereign Lord, what good will your reward do me, since I have no children? . . . and one of my slaves will inherit my property."

The Lord took him outside and said, "Look at the sky and try to count the stars; you will have as many descendants as that."

Abram put his trust in the Lord, and because of this the Lord was pleased with him and accepted him.

—Genesis 15:1-3, 5-6

Preparation: Pray this psalm after answering the question: "Whom do I trust?"

Read Psalm 119: (73-80) Read the quotation from Genesis carefully. Then read the eight verses from Psalm 119.

Reflection: Read these eight verses again, taking note of the statements that indicate the psalmist's trust of God. Does the author's trust have any conditions? How does your own trust of God compare? What do you think of this statement attributed to Eric Severeid: "Risk is what gives meaning to trust"? What risks is the psalmist willing to take? What risks are you willing to take?

Prayer: Begin your prayer with this phrase: "Because I trust in your promise . . . "

Psalm 119:81-88

"How much longer must I wait?"

> I am being driven forward
> Into an unknown land.
> The pass grows steeper,
> The air colder and sharper.
> A wind from my unknown goal
> Stirs the strings
> of expectation.
>
> Still the question:
> Shall I ever get there?
> There where life resounds,
> A clear pure note
> In the silence.[17]
> —DAG HAMMARSKJÖLD

Preparation: In preparation for this portion of Psalm 119, remember a time in your life, perhaps even now, when you have felt restless, marking time, waiting to be shown a new direction.

Read Psalm 119: Sense the mood of the writer as you read these verses.
(81-88)

Reflection: Have you ever felt as the writer of these verses felt? Have you felt called in a new direction but blocked in getting there? How does one wait patiently for God to show the way?

Prayer: Share your feelings with God . . . even your frustration and impatience. Listen.

Psalm 119:89-96

"I have learned that everything has limits"

Of course we would not dare classify ourselves or compare ourselves with those who rate themselves so highly. How stupid they are! They make up their own standards to measure themselves by, and they judge themselves by their own standards! As for us, however, our boasting will not go beyond certain limits; it will stay within the limits of the work which God has set for us. . . . We hope that your faith may grow and that we may be able to do a much greater work among you, always within the limits that God has set.

—2 Corinthians 10:12-13, 15-16

Preparation: In getting ready to pray this portion of the psalm, prepare to meet your limits!

Read Psalm 119: Read these verses very carefully to understand all that
(89-96) is being said.

Reflection: Do you think Paul and the author of Psalm 119 mean the same thing when they speak of "limits"? How does verse 96 follow from the preceding verses? What does it mean to "know one's limits"? Does it mean being restricted? Or does it give us freedom? How can you learn to be as comfortable with your limits as Paul and the psalmist seem to be?

Prayer: Pray for a knowledge of your limits and for the freedom that comes to those who know their limits.

Psalm 119:97-104

"For you have taught me" (NRSV)

Deep within us all there is an amazing inner sanctuary of the soul, a holy place, a Divine Center, a speaking Voice, to which we may continuously return. Eternity is at our hearts, pressing upon our time-torn lives, warming us with intimations of an astounding destiny, calling us home unto Itself. Yielding to these persuasions, gladly committing ourselves in body and soul, utterly and completely, to the Light Within, is the beginning of true life.[18]

—THOMAS R. KELLY

Preparation: In the stillness of your heart, listen for the voice within you which calls you home to Itself.

Read Psalm 119: (97-104) Read these verses twice as you feel the psalmist experienced them. Then read them a third time, focusing on how they relate to your own experience.

Reflection: Do verses 98-100 sound self-righteous to you? Is there another way to understand them? Is there a wisdom and even a conduct which is available to us because we are obedient to God's teachings? The psalmist says God is our teacher. Thomas Kelly says this God is a divine voice deep within us "to which we may continuously return."

Prayer: Can you offer God praise and thanksgiving for the benefits of hearing and following God's teaching . . . without being self-righteous?

Psalm 119:105-112

"Your word is a lamp to guide me"

> One thing I see in your light:
> this will, which you have given us as free,
> seems to receive its strength
> from the light of faith,
> for by this light
> we come in your light to know your eternal will,
> and we see that your will wants nothing else
> but that we be made holy.
>
> So the light strengthens the will
> and makes it grow,
> and the will,
> nourished by the light of holy faith,
> gives life to our human actions.[19]
> —CATHERINE OF SIENA

Preparation: Sit in a darkened room as you pray this psalm.
Read Psalm 119: Read the stanza and then return to the darkness for a
(105-112) few minutes before reading it again.
Reflection: Where is the "darkness" in *your* life? How have God's
teachings (laws, commands, etc.) served as light in
your life? How might you open the darkness of your
life to be "nourished by the light of holy faith"?
Prayer: Pray for the "light of holy faith" in *your* darkness.

Psalm 119:113-120

"I am filled with fear because of your judgments"

Humility is often confused with the gentlemanly self-deprecation of saying you're not much of a bridge player when you know perfectly well you are. Conscious or otherwise, this kind of humility is a form of gamesmanship.

If you really *aren't* much of a bridge player, you're apt to be rather proud of yourself for admitting it so humbly. This kind of humility is a form of low comedy.

True humility doesn't consist of thinking ill of yourself but of not thinking of yourself much differently from the way you'd be apt to think of anybody else. It is the capacity for being no more and no less pleased when you play your own hand well than when your opponents do.[20]

—FREDERICK BUECHNER

Preparation: What do you think it means to "fear God"?

Read Psalm 119: Read these verses carefully, noting especially the dif-
(113-120) ferent attitudes of the psalmist in verses 113 and 120.

Reflection: How did you *feel* when you read, "I hate those who are not completely loyal to you"? How did you *feel* when you read, "I am filled with fear because of your judgments"? Do you sometimes feel proud of your humility? Do you rejoice in the humility of others? What does it really mean "to fear God"?

Prayer: Ask God to help you understand these qualities.

Psalm 119:121-128

"My eyes are tired from watching for your saving help"

There are people who try to raise their souls like a man continually taking standing jumps in the hopes that, if he jumps higher every day, a time may come when he will no longer fall back but will go right up to the sky. Thus occupied he cannot look at the sky. We cannot take a single step toward heaven. It is not in our power to travel in a vertical direction. If however we look heavenward for a long time, God comes and takes us up. He raises us easily.[21]

—SIMONE WEIL

Preparation: How much time have you allowed for praying this psalm today? What would your reaction be if it took fifteen minutes more?

Read Psalm 119: (121-128) Read the eight verses. Then go back and read them again, noting any impatience expressed by the author.

Reflection: How many times have you said in your own prayer: "Lord, it is time for you to act"? It may be that God waits to answer our prayers until we cease being so anxious about them! What is it in you that wants instant answers to prayers (among other things)? Will the world end if your prayer is not answered on your own timetable? Can you learn to be more patient with God whose patience with you is boundless?

Prayer: Share your feelings with God and wait for God's answer.

Psalm 119:129-136

"My tears pour down like a river"

> The pain! I can't bear the pain!
> My heart! My heart is beating wildly!
> I can't keep quiet;
> I hear the trumpets and the shouts of battle.
> One disaster follows another;
> the whole country is left in ruins.
> —JEREMIAH 4:19-20a

Preparation: Remember a time when you were in pain because of a local or national policy that was particularly grievous to you.

Read Psalm 119: (129-136) Read these eight verses. Note the sudden shift in the last verse; read the passage again in the light of that verse.

Reflection: These verses are reminiscent of the pain of the prophets, who were so close to God that they dared to speak to the people in God's name. At the same time the verses are filled with pain because of the unfaithfulness of the people. Do you share that prophetic spirit? Do you have a vision of how things might be if only we were all obedient to God's teachings? Have you cried over the social, economic, and political mistakes of your nation because you could see the consequences when others couldn't?

Prayer: Pray to be made more sensitive to the call of both ancient and modern prophets.

Psalm 119:137-144

"I am unimportant and despised"

In these twenty years of work amongst the people, I have come more and more to realize that it is being unwanted that is the worst disease that any human being can ever experience. Nowadays we have found medicine for leprosy and lepers can be cured. There's medicine for TB and consumptives can be cured. For all kinds of diseases there are medicines and cures. But for being unwanted, except there are willing hands to serve and there's a loving heart to love, I don't think this terrible disease can ever be cured.[22]

—MOTHER TERESA OF CALCUTTA

Preparation: Think about someone you know or have heard about who is poor and powerless.

Read Psalm 119: Read this section of the psalm as a poor person might
(137-144) read it.

Reflection: Who are the "unimportant and despised" of our time? Do you know people who are thought of that way? What about our nation's treatment of minorities, migrant workers, and poor people? What about our policies toward third world people? What about your own attitudes? How do you feel when someone approaches you on the street asking for money or food? Can you step into the shoes of such persons for a few minutes to find out how *they* feel?

Prayer: Pray for forgiveness and for the ability to understand.

Psalm 119:145-152

"Before sunrise I call to you for help"

Now that we are about to lie down to sleep, grant us, O Master, the repose of our soul and body. Preserve us against the dark slumber of sin and against any impure satisfaction that roams around in the darkness of night; quiet the assaults of our passions, arrest the darts that the Evil One insidiously throws at us, still the commotions of our flesh, and calm all earthly and worldly feelings within us. Grant us, O Lord, a watchful mind, innocent thoughts, a sober heart, a gentle sleep free from evil dreams; at the hour of prayer, arouse us, strong in the practice of your commands and ever-mindful of your desires; give us the grace to sing your glory throughout the night; to praise, bless and glorify your all-honorable and magnificent name, Father, Son and Holy Spirit, now and always and for ever and ever. Amen. [23]

—CLOSING PRAYER FOR COMPLINE
BYZANTINE DAILY WORSHIP

Preparation:	Pray these verses just before going to bed at night.
Read Psalm 119:	Notice the references to the night hours.
(145-152)	
Reflection:	These verses are a reminder of the monastic "night office." Does not your bedtime prayer continue through the night? Perhaps you find yourself resuming your prayer if you awaken during the night or in the hour just before dawn.
Prayer:	Ask God to teach you to pray through the night.

Psalm 119:153-160

"Show your mercy and save me!"

Nothing that is worth doing can be achieved in our lifetime; therefore we must be saved by hope. Nothing which is true or beautiful or good makes complete sense in an immediate context of history; therefore we must be saved by faith. Nothing we do, however virtuous, can be accomplished alone; therefore we are saved by love. No virtuous act is quite as virtuous from the standpoint of our friend or foe as it is from our own standpoint. Therefore, we must be saved by the final form of love which is forgiveness.[24]

—REINHOLD NIEBUHR

Preparation: Before you pray these verses of the psalm, try to get in touch with your own need to be saved.

Read Psalm 119: (153-160) Read this section of the psalm once. Then go back and read it again, noticing the context of the author's repeated call upon God to "save me."

Reflection: Four times in eight verses, the psalmist says, "save me." While some of us may have more sophisticated or subtle ways of saying it, the need to be saved may well be the bottom line for all of us. Have you thought lately about what it is that you need to be saved from, to, and by means of?

Prayer: Read these verses again, letting them be the start of your own prayer asking God to save *you.*

Psalm 119:161-168

"... As happy as someone who finds a rich treasure"

The Kingdom of heaven is like this. A man happens to find a treasure hidden in a field. He covers it up again, and is so happy that he goes and sells everything he has, and then goes back and buys that field.
—MATTHEW 13:44

Preparation: Before you get ready to pray this part of Psalm 119, try to recall a time when you suddenly came into possession of a treasure and how you felt about it.

Read Psalm 119: (161-168) Read this section of Psalm 119. Then go back and read it again to note where the author feels happiness, thankfulness, security, and patience.

Reflection: Did you remember a time when you received a treasure, perhaps an inheritance, a generous gift, or a windfall? How did you feel? Have you ever felt that way about God's love, teachings, mercy, or promises? Reflect on how God's teachings are a treasure for you. What other non-material things are treasures in your life? Are you happy about such treasures? Are you thankful? How do they contribute to your security?

Prayer: Give thanks to God for all the treasures in your life.

Psalm 119:169-176

"I wander about like a lost sheep"

When Jesus got out of the boat, he saw this large crowd, and his heart was filled with pity for them, because they were like sheep without a shepherd. So he began to teach them many things.

—MARK 6:34

Preparation: Open yourself to feel what you think the author of this psalm may have felt writing the final verses.

Read Psalm 119: If you have prayed the other twenty-one sections of
(169-176) Psalm 119, read this one as a summary of all that has gone before.

Reflection: There is a sense in which Psalm 119 is a spiritual self-inventory. As you reflect on this closing section, what conclusions do you think the author came to? Have you ever had the feeling that you were wandering about "like a lost sheep" in spite of all your daily and weekly routines and disciplines? How do you think the people in the reading from Mark felt as they waited to hear Jesus speak to them? How do you think Jesus felt about them? How did their need and his teaching come together? How can you in your "wandering" open yourself to God's teaching?

Prayer: Can you pray with the psalmist:
"I wander about like a lost sheep;
   so come and look for me, your servant"?

Psalm 120

"I have lived too long with people who hate peace!"

Introduction: The fifteen "psalms of ascent" begin with Psalm 120. Various explanations have been given for this title which is used for each of the psalms. It is generally agreed that they were sung by pilgrims on their way to Jerusalem for one of the three great festivals (see Exodus 23:14-17 and Deuteronomy 16:16-17). The writer of Psalm 120 paints a contrast between Jerusalem and the regions of Meshech (far to the north near the Black Sea) and Kedar (a tribe of the Arabian Desert). Jerusalem is a place of peace in contrast to these far regions where the psalmist may have experienced cruelty.

Preparation: As you prepare to enter the quietness of praying this psalm, you may reflect on the contrast between this time of prayer and the frantic pace which often seems to rule our days.

Read Psalm 120: Read this brief psalm carefully, giving yourself time to translate it into your own experience. When you have done so, begin to pray it.

Reflection: Recall experiences you have had where you felt "all alone" in the midst of a crowd whose values seemed to be cruel, selfish, or prejudiced. Have you had the experience the psalmist speaks of: "When I speak of peace, they are for war"?

Prayer: Give thanks for your experience of peace in prayer and ask God to show you how to share it with others.

Psalm 121

"Your protector is always awake"

Introduction: Psalm 121 is the second of the gradual psalms or "songs of ascent" as they are called in their Hebrew titles. The meaning is uncertain. These psalms may have been used by pilgrims as they went up to Jerusalem. On the other hand, this may be a blessing given by a priest (verses 3-8) to a pilgrim about to leave on the journey home from Jerusalem. In any case it is an assurance of God's protection on a difficult journey.

Preparation: Prepare yourself for this journey of prayer into the presence of God.

Read Psalm 121: Read this beautiful psalm as if it were addressed to you personally on your own journey "up to Jerusalem."

Reflection: Recall a time when you were about to set out on a long and difficult journey, uncertain about what may lie ahead for you. Look again at Psalm 91 and compare its assurances of God's protection with those in this psalm. Notice the confidence of God's protection in these statements:
- "My help *will* come from the Lord"
- "He *will* not let you fall"
- "The Lord *will* guard you"
- "The Lord *will* protect you"

Prayer: Let the assurance of the psalm be addressed to you personally. Read it, changing *you* to *me*.

Psalm 122

"Pray for the peace of Jerusalem"

Introduction: For those who have visited Jerusalem, this psalm has special meaning. To read it is to relive your own journey! Verses 1-3 recount one's anticipation and arrival in Jerusalem; verses 4-5 celebrate the fact that peoples come to Jerusalem to give thanks and receive justice; finally verses 6-9 are a liturgical dialogue, but they also might be considered a blessing on the city offered by the departing pilgrim.

Preparation: Quietly center yourself to pray this psalm. Perhaps you can recall or anticipate a journey to the "city of peace."

Read Psalm 122: Read the psalm as if you were walking through one of the gates of the old city of Jerusalem.

Reflection: Late one night two friends and I arrived at the Ecce Homo Convent in the Old City of Jerusalem, tired from the long journey from the United States. When the clerk in the office offered us chairs, we hesitated, having been sitting for hours in planes, a bus, and a taxi. Understanding our reluctance, he said, "Ah, but *now* you are sitting in *Jerusalem!*" For how many centuries have pilgrims been praying for "the peace of Jerusalem"? And how many times has the "city of peace" been the victim of violence and destruction?

Prayer: Pray for the peace of Jerusalem and ask God to implant the spirit of Jerusalem in your heart.

Psalm 123

"We have been treated with so much contempt"

Introduction: When those who were exiles in Babylon were able to return to Israel, it was not the exciting experience seen by Isaiah (see Isaiah 40–55). Rather it was to a land of ruined cities and neglected friends. No doubt those who returned were mocked and ridiculed by those in neighboring countries. It was a time of discouragement and disappointment. In this communal lament, the people lift their eyes to God in humble obedience and hope (verses 1-2). The appeal to God is based, not on the righteousness of the people, but simply on their poverty of spirit.

Preparation: Before reading the psalm, reflect for a few moments on the conditions the people of Israel found when they returned from exile.

Read Psalm 123: Try to hear the words from the perspective of those who prayed it originally.

Reflection: Have you ever spent hours or weeks on a special project, only to have some thing happen to destroy it at the last moment? That is not unlike the feelings of those who first prayed this psalm.

Prayer: Can you pray this statement? "As a servant depends on his master, as a maid depends on her mistress, so we will keep looking to you, O Lord our God."

Psalm 124

"What if the Lord had not been on our side?"

Introduction: This thanksgiving for national deliverance may be an adaptation of an earlier psalm relating to an individual rescue. Verses 2-5 may refer to the kind of flood which roars down from the mountains following a sudden rainstorm, or it may refer to the people of Israel passing safely through the Red Sea. Whatever the original event, the psalm is a deeply felt thanksgiving for those who have been spared from a sudden life-threatening situation. The concluding line, "Our help comes from the Lord, who made heaven and earth" is often used as a versicle in Christian worship.

Preparation: As you center yourself to pray this psalm, you may want to have in mind an experience in which you were personally confronted with great danger and narrowly escaped.

Read Psalm 124: Read the psalm the first time to become familiar with its imagery and flow of feelings. Then read it again as your own personal prayer of thanksgiving for having been rescued from a great danger.

Reflection: Whether or not we believe that God breaks into history to rescue us from danger, we often feel that we have been protected or guided by someone outside ourselves when we realize how close we have come to death or injury.

Prayer: Pray the psalm, substituting your name for that of the nation; add your own feelings as you continue your prayer.

Psalm 125

"As the mountains surround Jerusalem"

Introduction: Another of the "gradual" or "pilgrim" psalms, this is a song of trust that those who are faithful to the commands of the Lord will inherit the land of Zion and live securely in it. We can imagine it being sung by pilgrims who have seen with their own eyes the way the Jerusalem is surrounded by mountains. "So the Lord surrounds his people, now and forever." The assurance that "the wicked will not always rule over the land of the righteous" may be a response to anxiety about whether God would honor the promise to restore Zion after the time of exile.

Preparation: Do you give yourself adequate time to become centered before reading and praying the psalms? Do you feel anxious about the time? If so, you might do well to ask yourself how important time for prayer is to you. If it is a high priority, then it should be given not only *enough* time, but enough *quality* time.

Read Psalm 125: Imagine yourself in Jerusalem surrounded by the mountains. Read the psalm in this perspective.

Reflection: Is your "trust in the Lord" such that you cannot be shaken? How do you feel about verse 3? Are you tempted to "do evil" because others around you are "wicked"?

Prayer: What feelings and thoughts does this psalm raise in you? Share your feelings, thoughts, and questions with God.

Psalm 126

"As the rain brings water back to dry riverbeds"

Introduction: This is a psalm recalling the joyous return from the exile. The first three verses recall the sheer joy and exhilaration of coming home from Babylon. In the Hebrew, verse 1 can also be read "when the Lord returned with the captives," in which case the return takes on the character of a liturgical procession. But merely being back in the land of promise is not enough. There is work to be done. Verse 5 invokes the presence of God as the people restore the land. In verse 6 is the promise that the sorrow and labor of planting will be rewarded with the joy of the harvest.

Preparation: As you prepare yourself for praying this psalm, remember the joy of those who returned from exile, but also the work they faced to restore the land.

Read Psalm 126: Read the psalm as if you were there when it was written, after the first crops were planted, but before the harvest.

Reflection: What is it in your life that you yearn to return to, "as rain brings water back to dry riverbeds"? What have you planted in your life with tears, which has yet to bloom or ripen?

Prayer: Give thanks to God for the opportunity to plant and for God's steadfast love, which is with you as you await the harvest.

Psalm 127

" . . . Eating the bread of anxious toil" (NRSV)

Introduction: This is not one of the psalms used in the liturgy of the Temple, but rather an example of a more "earthy" wisdom. In its present form it may represent fragments of two earlier bits of wisdom literature (verses 1-2 and 3-5) held together by a common theme of the vanity of human efforts without God. The meanings seem somewhat obscured, and it might be helpful to compare more than one translation to get the flavor, especially in verse 2.

Preparation: Our prayer life can be greatly enhanced by experimenting to find a good time and place every day. Is there a good *time*, even a few minutes, which you can set aside each day? What *place* feels right for prayer?

Read Psalm 127: Note the different "gems of wisdom" in verse 1, verse 2, and verses 4-5.

Reflection: What place does God have in your "building projects"? Do you "eat the bread of anxious toil" (verse 2, NRSV)? What does the psalmist mean by, "The Lord provides for those he loves, *while they are asleep*" (verse 2)?

Prayer: Share your feelings and insights with God. Ask God to help you to make your toil less anxious.

Psalm 130

"Out of the depths I cry to you, O Lord" (NRSV)

Introduction: This psalm is known to many by its opening words in Latin, *De profundis*—out of the depths. It is the classic penitential psalm. One can imagine the psalmist awake in the night or perhaps keeping a vigil in the Temple, waiting for the Lord's help, more eagerly than watchmen wait for the dawn. It is both a powerful statement of the human condition and a joyful acknowledgment of God's love, which is stronger than death. It is one of the most magnificent statements of faith in the Psalter, declaring profound hope, even in the midst of profound despair.

Preparation: As we prepare for prayer, it is not necessary to ask for God to be present to us. It is only necessary to put aside our distractions so that *we can be present to God* who is already as close as our breath.

Read Psalm 130: This is a psalm worth reading again and again, perhaps in different translations. Read it and pray it, until finally, the psalm prays itself.

Reflection: "From the depths of my despair" (TEV). Rare is the person who has not been there. Recall a time of your own despair. What feelings did you have about God as you struggled through it? Anger? Abandonment? Apathy?

Prayer: Pray for the gift of being open to God's presence in your life, even when you cry "out of the depths."

Psalm 131

"As a child lies quietly in its mother's arms"

Introduction: Another gem of the Psalter, Psalm 131, is a song of trust. Such songs originally followed a lament. After a favorable response to an appeal for God's help came a sense of gratitude. Here the psalmist gives up any pretense of self-sufficiency in order to be fully open to the grace of God. The sense of trust and contentment is conveyed in the image of the child lying quietly in its mother's arms. The Hebrew is even stronger, meaning the contentment of the child with a full stomach remaining quietly at its mother's breast. The RSV renders the phrase: "like a child quieted at its mother's breast."

Preparation: As you begin to center yourself, let not only the thoughts and cares of the day drift away from you, but also the need to provide for yourself in this special time. Open yourself completely and totally to God's grace.

Read Psalm 131:   Take plenty of time in your reading of this brief psalm. Linger over every phrase.

Reflection: What would it be like to give up your pride and turn away from your arrogance? Can you relax enough to be simple, even childlike?

Prayer: Ask God to help you learn how to be so simple and trusting that you can be like a child in its mother's arms.

Psalm 132

"I will not rest or sleep until I provide a place for the Lord"

Introduction: Psalm 132 is a liturgical psalm about King David's bringing of the ark of the covenant to the Temple. Verses 1-5 recall David's struggle to conquer Jerusalem. Verses 6-7 are perhaps a response by the worshipers who remember the discovery of the ark and its being brought to a sanctuary in Jerusalem while the Temple was being built. Verses 8-9 are prayers for the priests and people as they arrive at the Temple. The remainder of the psalm helps us remember God's promise to David and blessing to the people.

Preparation: As we go about our daily tasks we are seldom aware of the energy and tension (in a positive sense) we expend in order to function mentally and physically. As a result, our spiritual being tends to be neglected. Centering and praying scripture offer us a time to relax these necessary tensions in order to give attention to our *spiritual* growth.

Read Psalm 132: Read the psalm carefully, paying attention to its various parts.

Reflection: Reflect on the words ascribed to David in the psalm: "I will not rest or sleep until I provide a place for the Lord." Does providing a place for God have a priority in your life? What are the priorities in your life each day? each week?

Prayer: Ask God to help you make any needed changes which could enhance your spiritual life.

Psalm 133

"Like the dew on Mount Hermon"

Introduction: Psalm 133 has its roots in the economic and cultural practices of ancient Israel. Property, held in trust as the Lord's gift, was passed on at the death of the head of household to the oldest son. The younger brothers with their families then came under the headship of the eldest. Strained relationships in the extended family were not unusual. The psalm is thus a blessing over a family in crisis. The metaphors of the precious oil and the dew watering crops in a dry season suggest the role of the elder brother, who was the source of blessings to his siblings (compare to the role of the king in Psalm 72). The family then becomes a metaphor for all of God's people.

Preparation: Ask God to help you be fully present to this prayer.

Read Psalm 133: Read this psalm two or three times, reflecting on different "family" experiences you have had. Take time to savor the rich imagery of the family in harmony, an ideal we may not always match, but which remains a worthy goal.

Reflection: Have you experienced this blessing in your own family life? If not, what could you do to help your family (or another family) taste it? How can you make this vision available to your neighborhood, your school, or your church?

Prayer: Share with God your feelings about your own experience of family. What do you feel called to do?

Psalm 135

"Whatever the Lord pleases . . . " (NRSV)

Introduction: This liturgical hymn begins and ends with an invitation to Israel to praise the Lord, telling God's story to the world (verses 1-4). The power of God over nature is recited in verses 5-7, followed by a brief remembrance of God's liberating activity in the Exodus event. The Lord's defeat of hostile powers means that idols representing those powers are worthless. These four verses about idols are repeated in Psalm 115:4-8. The psalm closes with a call for people, priests, Levites, and all who worship to bless the Lord in Jerusalem.

Preparation: Ask yourself: "Why do I want to pray?" When you are satisfied with your answer, prepare your spirit to pray this psalm.

Read Psalm 135: Read the psalm once; then go back and read it again using verses 5-18 as a basis for your reflection.

Reflection: Think about the phrase, "Whatever the Lord pleases he does." Do you feel the same way about God bringing "storm clouds from the ends of the earth" (verse 7, TEV) as you do about God killing "all the first-born of [humans] and animals (verse 8, TEV)"? In the Psalms people often seem to be telling God what to do. What about your own prayers? Are you really comfortable with praying, "*Thy* will be done"? Do you try to tell God what to do, or do you allow God to be God?

Prayer: Ask God to help you to be more honest in your prayers and more open to God's will and ways.

Psalm 136

"[God's] love is eternal"

Introduction: While Psalms 113–118 are known as the *Hallel* (praise) psalms, Psalm 136 is called the "Great *Hallel*." Opening with praise for the goodness of God, the psalm moves in verses 4-9 to a celebration of God as Creator, and then in verses 10-22 to a remembrance of the Exodus story. The closing verses offer thanks for God's continuing care for Israel. As the form suggests, the verses of the psalm were quite likely sung by a priest with the congregation responding "his love is eternal" after each verse. Some may prefer "his steadfast love endures forever" (NRSV) or "his mercy endures forever" (NAB).

Preparation: As you prepare to pray this psalm, you might remember that the individual verses were sung by a priest or cantor, after each of which the congregation responded with praise to God.

Read Psalm 136: Read the psalm first to become aware of the flow of ideas in the verses. Then pray it using the response after each verse.

Reflection: As you pray this psalm try to be aware of the great Exodus tradition behind it and be thankful for the recalling of that part of our Judeo-Christian heritage. Can you think of another series of verses for this psalm that celebrate God's guidance and care for your own personal journey?

Prayer: Let your prayer flow out of your reflection, adding your own special reasons for giving thanks to God.

Psalm 137

"How could we sing the Lord's song in a foreign land?" (NRSV)

<table>
<tr><td>Introduction:</td><td>Psalm 137 dates from the time when the exiles returned to Jerusalem from Babylon. Having witnessed the destruction of Jerusalem, they recall the pain of being asked by their captors to entertain with happy songs about Zion. Now back in Jerusalem, the singers remember their resolve never to forget their home. Verse 7 is a reference to the betrayal of the Edomites who collaborated with the Babylonians in the capture of Jerusalem. Verses 8-9 provide more than adequate testimony to the bitterness felt by those who returned. While these words are terrible to modern ears, we might remind ourselves that it is better to vent our anger in words than in deeds.</td></tr>
<tr><td>Preparation:</td><td>When you are ready to read the psalm, you might begin by asking yourself this question: How do those of us Paul called "citizens of heaven" (Phil. 3:20) sing the Lord's song in a foreign land called earth?</td></tr>
<tr><td>Read Psalm 137:</td><td>Read the psalm seeking to understand the feelings of those who experienced the Babylonian captivity.</td></tr>
<tr><td>Reflection:</td><td>How do we who are citizens of heaven sing the Lord's song in a world of greed, pollution, prejudice, and weapons of mass destruction? What do we do to express our bitterness toward those who rape God's creation for profit?</td></tr>
<tr><td>Prayer:</td><td>Ask God to teach us how to sing "new songs" which will change our hearts and those of our captors.</td></tr>
</table>

Psalm 138

"You care for the lowly"

Introduction:	Few psalms can match the simple trust and humility found in Psalm 138. Out of God's mercy the prayer of the psalmist has been heard. God who is "high above" still cares for the lowly. It is a deeply personal psalm.
Preparation:	Take whatever time is necessary to distance yourself from the problems and agenda of your day. Remember God's gracious care for you.
Read Psalm 138:	This psalm is filled with phrases which call us to humility and praise. Read it quietly and very slowly, savoring every line.
Reflection:	Spend a few minutes meditating on each of the following:

- *"I thank you, Lord, with all my heart"* (verse 1)
- *"You answered me when I called to you"* (verse 3)
- *"With your strength you stengthened me"* (verse 3)
- *You care for the lowly, and the proud cannot hide from you"* (verse 6)
- *"Complete the work that you have begun"* (verse 8)

Prayer:	Let your prayer begin with one or more of the thoughts to which you said yes in this experience.

Psalm 139

"Even before I speak . . . "

Introduction: A favorite of many, Psalm 139 is perhaps the most personal and at the same time the most philosophical of the psalms. Written in a meditative style, it reflects first in verses 1-6 on God's complete knowledge of the psalmist; then in verses 7-12 on God's presence everywhere; and finally in verses 13-16*a* on God's creative power. Verses 16*b*-18 summarize the wonder of all that has been said before. Then, suddenly, as if waking up from this pleasant reflection, the psalmist remembers that the world is also peopled with those who do not respect the ways of God. The contrast of verses 19-22 is almost like an intrusion into the text. This recalling of sin ends as abruptly as it began, and the psalm closes with a petition for God to "examine me . . . test me . . . guide me."

Preparation: Setting aside other thoughts and agendas, open yourself for a very intimate encounter with God.

Read Psalm 139: You may find it helpful the first time you pray this psalm to omit verses 19-22. But even these harsh words have something to teach us at another time.

Reflection: The psalm is filled with the wonder of God's knowledge, presence, and power. Which phrases call forth that sense of wonder in you, personally? How do you feel about the God who created you, knows you, and is always present to you?

Prayer: Try to pray the two closing verses with complete openness to God.

Psalm 141

"Lord, place a guard at my mouth"

Introduction: This psalm, like many others, reflects on those who are good and those who are evil. The author prays to be included among the good rather than the evil, whose bones will be scattered like chips of wood when a log is split. Even punishment is to be accepted if it comes from the good, but not from those who are evil. The psalmist asks the Lord to "place a guard at my mouth" knowing how easy it is for all of us to find ourselves speaking in jealousy and anger. In monastic prayer, incense is often lighted as verse 2 of this psalm is read. The translation of verses 6-7 from the Hebrew is difficult and uncertain. For the purpose of our prayer, the psalm is probably better without them.

Preparation: One of the thoughts behind this psalm is the value of silence when we are tempted to speak unwisely. Prepare yourself to pray it with real silence.

Read Psalm 141: Read the psalm, omitting verses 6-7 if you prefer.

Reflection: How often do you blurt out something and almost instantly regret having said it? How can the discipline of silence keep us from doing wrong?

Prayer: Let your prayer rise before God "as incense," with a new appreciation of silence.

Psalm 142

"When I am ready to give up"

Introduction: This psalm is a simple and direct prayer on the part of one who has been forsaken, persecuted, and brought to the depths of despair. Whether real or metaphorical, the author feels shut up in prison like Jeremiah. There is no one to help or care. Yet, having apparently received assurance from a priest, the psalmist continues in prayer calling to God for help. Lifted by the possibility of God's action, the petitioner ends the prayer on a note of confidence and a promise to offer praise to God in the assembly of the people.

Preparation: Can you simply open yourself to God in this time of prayer? Can you trust in God who "knows what I should do"?

Read Psalm 142: If you can remember a time when you felt forsaken by others or were without friends to help you, read the psalm in the light of your own experience.

Reflection: "When I am ready to give up, [God] knows what I should do." Most of us know all too well that we feel little need of God when things are going well in our lives. We want to think of ourselves as independent and self-sufficient. That is why we usually feel embarrassed asking for God's help when we are down. What would it take for us to seek God's help when things are going *well* for us?

Prayer: Ask God to help you toward a greater maturity out of which you can ask for guidance in *all* circumstances.

Psalm 143

"My soul thirsts for you like a parched land" (NRSV)

Introduction:	Psalm 143 has long been recognized as one of the great penitential psalms. The psalmist has been the victim of evil people, and as a result has been left in darkness, "ready to give up." Yet, remembering how God has rescued people in the past, the author pleads to be delivered from those who have made life so miserable. The genuine humility of the psalmist is evident throughout.
Preparation:	After you have prepared yourself to pray this psalm, recall a time in your life when things seemed hopeless.
Read Psalm 143:	Read the psalm very slowly, allowing the full meaning of each line to penetrate to the depths of your own spirit. Then read it a second time, allowing the psalm to pray itself in you.
Reflection:	The psalmist says: "I am ready to give up . . . I have lost all hope." Do you think that is really true? Notice the action verbs in the petitions to God: "answer me," "remind me," "show me," "teach me," "rescue me."
Prayer:	Give thanks to God for hope in the midst of what seems so hopeless, for glimmers of light when all seems to be so very dark.

Psalm 145

"The Lord is loving and merciful"

Introduction: This psalm is another alphabetic acrostic in form. It borrows from several other psalms (15, 58, 86, 103, and 104) and as a result does not highly develop any of its own themes. But, what it may lack in literary style, it makes up for in its understanding of the compassion of God. The great theme of this psalm, stated in verse 8, is found in Exodus 34:6 and Numbers 14:18. "The Lord is loving and merciful, slow to become angry and full of constant love."

Preparation: As you settle into the quietness needed for meditation, know that there is nothing ponderous in this psalm. It is rather a hymn of unrestrained joy and thanksgiving for the love and compassion of God.

Read Psalm 145: Read this psalm, knowing that it offers a myriad of reasons for giving thanks and praise to God. It is to be heard as the sum of its many parts, yet every thought stands alone and is worthy of reflection.

Reflection: Notice the emphasis on our *future* response to the love of God which is based on the *present* action of God. Note also that every verse except 2, 10, and 21 contains a new reason for praising God's love and care for the people.

Prayer: Can you praise God for all these reasons? What other reasons would you add?

Psalm 146

"No human being can save you"

Introduction: In Psalms 146–150 we have another series of *Hallel* (praise) psalms, each beginning and ending with the words "Praise the Lord." Psalm 146 provided the inspiration for Isaac Watts' hymn, "I'll Praise My Maker While I've Breath." It paints a vivid contrast between human leaders whose "plans come to an end" when they die and "the Creator of heaven, earth, and sea," who "keeps promises, judges in favor of the oppressed and gives food to the hungry." Happy are those who depend upon God.

Preparation: For centuries the liturgy of Ash Wednesday has included the words: "Remember that you are dust and to dust you will return." Try to sense this perspective on your own humanness.

Read Psalm 146: Read the psalm twice, noting the feelings which are evoked by it.

Reflection: Read the text of Isaac Watt's great hymn, "I'll Praise My Maker While I've Breath," in the same way you read the psalm. What do you think of the psalmist's view of human leaders? How do you stack up as a human leader?

Prayer: In your prayer, try to put your own feelings about human efforts in perspective. Ask God to help you and others to be more sensitive to the needs of oppressors and the oppressed.

Psalm 147

"[The Lord] spreads snow like a blanket"

Introduction:	This "hallelujah" psalm offers praise to God as the Creator of the universe and as the Savior of Israel. The first section (verses 1-6) calls on the people to praise God, who has brought back the exiles and is restoring Jerusalem. In part two (verses 7-11) God is praised as the one who provides food for the animals and who delights not in war horses and soldiers, but in those who trust in God's steadfast love. The final section calls upon Jerusalem to praise the God who protects her people and even directs the weather. While the three parts blend together into one great hymn of praise, they have been joined from separate sources.
Preparation:	Following an opening "hallelujah" (Praise the Lord), the psalm reminds us that it is "good," "pleasant," and "right" to offer praise. In addition to preparing your quiet space, reflect a moment on these reasons for praying the psalms.
Read Psalm 147:	Read the psalm slowly as a whole; then go back and read each of the three sections, pausing to meditate on each.
Reflection:	How many reasons do you find in this psalm for praising God? Can you make a litany out of the verbs the psalmist uses to describe God's actions?
Prayer:	Try to summarize each of the three parts of the psalm as you offer praise to God.

Psalm 148

"Let them all praise the name of the Lord!"

Introduction: Psalm 148 is a hymn of creation, inviting both heaven and earth to sing praise. Part I calls upon the heavenly creation (verses 1-2) and heavenly phenomena (verses 3-4). Then follows a refrain (verses 5-6) sung by the Temple choir. Part II is addressed to the earthly creation made of "the deep" and things that arise from it (verses 7-8), the earth and things on it (verses 9-10), and the people of the earth (verses 11-12). A second refrain follows in verses 13-14a.

Preparation: No somber moods today! This psalm is a hymn of unrestrained joy. Prepare to celebrate!

Read Psalm 148: Read the psalm the first time, noting the different orders of creation. Then after a brief silence, go back and "sing" it as the great hymn of praise it is.

Reflection: Compare the biblical text of the psalm with the great hymn, "Praise the Lord! Ye Heavens Adore Him." Compare this psalm with Psalm 104. Which do you prefer? Why?

Prayer: Let your prayer be your own hymn of praise to the God of creation. Add those created things for which you are most thankful.

Psalm 149

"The Lord takes pleasure in the chosen people" (AP)

Introduction: Scholars often debate the date and circumstances of Psalm 149. Some feel it was composed as early as 300 B.C.E., while others cite a tradition relating it to the time of the Maccabees. What seems like a rupture of thematic continuity in the middle of verse 6 is part of the problem. A possible answer may be in God's honoring of the humble (verse 4) and commanding that nations be punished and kings be bound in chains (verse 8). The psalm carries the sense of the celebration of a military victory, while there are still more battles to be fought.

Preparation: Sometimes the scriptures almost seem to pray themselves as we read them. Other times, either because the passage is difficult or we are in a bad place personally, *lexio* becomes a formidable task. The important thing is that we open ourselves and remain faithful to the process.

Read 149: This is not an easy psalm to understand or to pray. We will need to be open to the leading of the words and the Spirit and cautious about drawing firm conclusions.

Reflection: The juxtaposition of themes in verses 4 and 8 is such that we can't help but be reminded of the revolutionary theology of Mary's song of praise found in Luke 1:52: "[God] has brought down mighty kings from their thrones, and lifted up the lowly."

Prayer: Give thanks to God for the Word, which surprises and delights us with the unexpected. Pray for those who are oppressed.

Psalm 150

"Praise the Lord, all living creatures!"

Introduction: Here in all its brevity and simplicity is the grand finale of the Psalter. It is not hard to imagine a celebration with orchestra, chorus, dancers, and fireworks all offering praise to the Lord together. The TEV calls upon "all living creatures" to praise the Lord. A better translation of the Hebrew would be "everything that breathes" (NRSV). The word for breath and spirit is the same, not only in Hebrew, but also in Greek and Latin. Psalm 104:30 says, "when you give them breath, they are created." Thus it is with the life (breath, spirit) that God has given us that we offer our praise.

Preparation: As you get ready to pray this last psalm, take several slow, deep breaths, remembering that our breath is God's spirit within us.

Read Psalm 150: Do not read this psalm silently. Give it breath and spirit. Sing it! Shout it! Hallelujah! Praise the Lord!

Reflection: If you have the opportunity, choose a favorite piece of music to help you praise the Lord. Praise the Lord with your "breath," which is God's own spirit!

Prayer: Praise God for psalms. Praise God for your very breath. Praise God for prayer.

APPENDIX A

Types of

Psalms

*Lord, every day I call to you
and lift my hands to you in prayer.*

Psalm 88:9

Why the Psalms?

Why has this book focused on the Psalms rather than other parts of the Hebrew and Christian scripture? Simply because one has to start someplace, and what better place to start than with what both Jews and Christians have long regarded as the "prayer book of the Bible." Most of the Psalms were originally intended either as individual prayers or as liturgical prayers for use by the community of worshipers in the Temple in Jerusalem. Indeed many of the Psalms were first written as individual prayers and later adapted to the Temple liturgy.

If you have begun by praying the Psalms and are comfortable with them, then it is very easy to begin praying one of the Gospels or part of the Book of Isaiah or perhaps one of Paul's letters. Then you will discover that you can pray almost any part of the Bible. There are some exceptions, of course. The genealogies found in Genesis and in the Gospel of Matthew do not make very interesting material for prayer!

Our spiritual ancestors in Israel worshiped mostly in local synagogues, but there was also the sacrificial worship in the Temple in Jerusalem. All of the faithful were expected to make a journey to Jerusalem to participate in the Temple services. The Psalms were not only used in worship, but they speak about worship. They speak about the joy of going to worship in the Temple (Psalm 122), about the duty of worship (Psalms 26 and 40), and about the desire to worship in the Temple (Psalm 84).

A Variety of Types and Themes

The Psalms as we know them came originally from many different times and sources. In addition many of them were edited, divided, combined, or otherwise adapted for use in different situations. As such the Psalms address many topics and situations. A few examples will suffice to illustrate the wide variety of topics covered by psalms intended for use by individuals: grief and depression (Psalm 6); illness (Psalm 31); thanksgiving for being spared from death (Psalm 30); reflection on good and evil (Psalm 37); exile (Psalms 42 and 43); a reflection on money (Psalm 49); awareness of sin (Psalm 51); longing for God (Psalm 63); sanctuary from enemies (Psalm 71); the brevity of life (Psalm 90); anger and bitterness (Psalm 109); and security in God (Psalm 131).

Likewise there are many themes to be found in the corporate psalms, some of which were adapted for community use from earlier individual prayers: wisdom psalms (Psalms 34, 37, 49, 73, 107); historical psalms (78, 105, 106); pilgrimage psalms (84, 120–134); psalms related to the king (72, 101, 144); covenant psalms (81, 111); God in nature (8, 29, 65, 147, 148); the law of the Lord (19:7-14, 119); Jerusalem or Zion (46, 48, 87); God's justice (7, 72, 75, 96).

Because the Psalms address so many aspects of human experience, many scholars have found it helpful to divide them into various types or categories, some more successfully than others. Some, like Donald Griggs,[25] choose to divide the Psalms into numerous types:

Praise and Thanksgiving	Individual Laments
Creation	Community Laments

Salvation History   Trust
The Lord as King   Torah
Hymns of Zion   Wisdom
Royal   Liturgical

Most scholars, however, use broader categories. Artur Weiser,[26] for example, names five types:

Hymns   Blessing and Curse
Laments   Wisdom and Didactic
Thanksgivings

Richard J. Clifford[27] offers three main genres of Psalms:

Psalms of Lament
Thanksgiving Psalms
Hymns

A more thematic system is suggested by Erik Routley:[28]

Suffering   Care
Victory   The City
Covenant   Faith
Praise   Life's Stress
Pilgrimage   Wisdom
Royalty   Character
Nature

George Appleton in his *Understanding the Psalms* offers a way of looking at the Psalms thematically.[29] His "Index of Themes" provides a number of sub-themes under three major headings:

God in the Psalms
Man in the Psalms
Israel in the Psalms

Perhaps the most creative approach to classifying the Psalms is that of Walter Bruggemann:[30]

APPENDIX A

Psalms of Orientation
Psalms of Disorientation
Psalms of New Orientation

Obviously no single system of categorizing the Psalms is without limitations. Nevertheless, it is helpful to be familiar with several ways of recognizing different kinds of psalms. Simply having a broad overview of various types is helpful to anyone who cares to pray them or study them further. A psalm, like any other reading from the Bible, is better understood if we know something about its history, purpose, and style.

Volumes have also been written about the literary style of the Psalms. Approaching the Psalms from that perspective provides additional ways of typing them. While it has not been within the purpose of this book to examine the Psalms from the point of view of their literary style, it may be of interest to look briefly at four types of literary parallelism found in the Psalter. A few minutes spent in becoming familiar with these types of parallelism will enhance one's appreciation of the Psalms as they are read and prayed. The following examples will suffice to provide such an overview.

Synonymous parallelism: The main thought of one line is repeated or added to in the following line.

> *Praise the Lord, my soul!*
> *All my being, praise his holy name!*   (103:1)

> *We have sinned as our ancestors did;*
> *we have been wicked and evil.*   (106:6)

> *You see me, whether I am working or resting;*
> *you know all my actions.*   (139:3)

Synthetic parallelism: The second line adds something new to the first line.

> *But he sent a man ahead of them,*
> *Joseph, who had been sold as a slave.*   (105:17)

> *Don't abandon me to my enemies,*
> *who attack me with lies and threats.*   (27:12)

[202]

Sing praises to the Lord!
Play music on the harps! (98:5)

Antithetic parallelism: The second line says the opposite of the first line.

My father and mother may abandon me,
    but the Lord will take care of me. (27:10)

Those who are blessed by the Lord will
    possess the land,
but those who are cursed by him will
    be driven out. (37:22)

You were good to me, Lord; you protected me
    like a mountain fortress.
But, then you hid yourself from me,
    and I was afraid. (30:7)

Comparative parallelism: One line expresses a thought in comparison to the other or uses a metaphor to explain the other line.

As far as the east is from the west,
so far does he remove our sins from us. (103:12)

There they were seized with fear and anguish,
like a woman about to bear a child. (48:6)

As the mountains surround Jerusalem,
so the Lord surrounds his people, now and forever. (125:2)

Those who would like to explore the Psalms in greater depth may wish to refer to the books listed in the bibliography at the end of this volume.

APPENDIX B

Praying
Other Parts
of the
Bible

If you have found praying the Psalms to be a helpful way of enhancing your own prayer life, you may want to continue in this traditional practice by using other parts of the Bible. You can begin with some of the passages recommended below, or you may want to choose one book or part of a book, such as the Sermon on the Mount, and pray your way through it.

When you pray other parts of the Bible, you may find passages that describe a particular situation or tell a story, such as the story of Jesus at the home of Mary and Martha at Bethany or any of the stories of encounters which took place between Jesus and others. As you begin your reflection on such passages, allow yourself to set the scene in your mind. Imagine what the place might have looked like, who else was there, and so forth. Assign yourself a role in the scene. You might choose to be the person being addressed by Jesus, or you may simply want to be one of those who happened to be present and thus allow yourself to observe the action from that perspective. Let your mind be creative.

As you continue in your reflection on the passage, pay attention to your feelings. As you read it a second time, there will likely be a phrase that seems to stand out for you. Learn to recognize these phrases, and allow them to become the focus of your reflection just like the theme phrases which were used in the psalm meditations. Let your mind play with the phrase. Ask yourself what it meant in its original context, what it means for you, what it might be saying to you, and why it seems to lift itself out for you.

Here are some passages you may find helpful as you begin to pray other parts of the Bible:

Deuteronomy 1:6-8	Luke 7:36-50
Joshua 1:1-9	Luke 9:18-20
Isaiah 43:1-5	Luke 9:57-62
Isaiah 55:1-3	Luke 10:21-24
Isaiah 55:6-9	Luke 10:38-42
Isaiah 55:10-11	Luke 11:5-13
Isaiah 58:6-12	Luke 11:33-36
Matthew 5:21-26	Luke 12:13-21
Matthew 6:5-6	Luke 12:22-31
Matthew 6:14-15	Luke 12:32-34
Matthew 6:19-21	Luke 12:35-40
Matthew 6:24-34	Luke 12:41-48
Matthew 7:1-6	Luke 12:49-53
Mark 7:31-37	Luke 12:54-56
Luke 1:46-55	Luke 13:1-5
Luke 4:31-37	Luke 13:31-35
Luke 5:27-32	Luke 14:7-14
Luke 6:27-36	Luke 14:25-33
Luke 6:37-38	Luke 15:11-32
Luke 6:43-45	Luke 17:1-4
Luke 6:47-49	

Soon you will discover that almost any passage of scripture will lend itself to your praying it if you are open to hear what it is saying to you.

APPENDIX C

Index of

Meditation

Themes

(Numbers refer to Psalms, not pages)

Angels
  34, 91
Anger (bitterness, etc.)
  13, 35, 39, 44, 58, 62, 76, 109, 137
Anxiety (see also: Stress)
  39, 54, 116, 119:121-128, 127, 142

Community
  2, 72, 80
Confession
  12, 32, 36, 38, 39, 51, 59, 85, 106,
  130
Confidence
  16, 41, 46, 57
Creation (nature)
  8, 19a, 24, 29, 33, 62, 65, 93, 96,
  98, 104, 119:33-40, 125, 147, 148

Darkness
  119:105-112
Death
  30, 39, 49, 71, 88, 90, 116
Discouragement (despair, depression)
  22, 31, 34, 40, 69, 74, 79, 116,
  119:25-32, 119:137-144, 119:169-176,
  123, 130, 137, 142, 143
Doubt
  22

Enemies
  3, 5, 10, 17, 35, 54, 55, 57, 59, 80,
  109
Evening
  31, 92
Evil
  5, 10, 36, 37, 54, 58, 73, 125, 141